Build Your Own Computer

2nd Edition

D1732662

Kenneth L. Hughes

Wordware Publishing, Inc.

Library of Congress Cataloging-in-Publication Data

Hughes, Kenneth L.
    Build your own computer / Kenneth L. Hughes. -- 2nd ed.
      p. cm.
    Includes index.
    ISBN 1-55622-459-1
    1. Microcomputers--Design and construction--Amateurs' manuals.
    I. Title.
    TK9969.H84   1995
    621.39'16--dc20   95-14627
                                                CIP

ISBN1-55622-459-1

10 9 8 7 6 5 4 3 2 1

9505

Microsoft is a registered trademark and Windows and the Windows Logo are trademarks
of Microsoft Corporation.
Other product names mentioned are used for identification purposes only and may be
trademarks of their respective companies.

All inquiries for volume purchases of this book should be addressed to
Wordware Publishing, Inc., at the above address. Telephone inquiries may be
made by calling:

(214) 423-0090

Contents

List of Illustrations

Figures

Tables

Section 1

About This Book

Introduction

This second edition of *Build Your Own Computer* has become necessary because of the great technological advances that have been made since its first printing. However, the organization of the book has not been materially changed and still allows individuals, private or corporate, with little or no technical knowledge of computers to gain sufficient understanding of the subject to enable them to assemble a complete "state-of-the-art" computer system. But the book does not end there, leaving the inexperienced reader to figure out how to use the computer. Information is also provided so that in conjunction with user manuals supplied with hardware and software, a newcomer can readily become productive. A section called "DOS For Beginners" is included, but it has been placed at the end so as not to impede the natural progression of the book for those who understand DOS.

There is much to learn about the subject of computers, but, if the application programs you intend to run on your computer are no more advanced than those used by a data entry clerk, then in-depth knowledge is not a vital necessity. However, having made the decision to build a computer rather than to purchase an assembled one, most readers are likely to also look for in-depth knowledge, and such information is provided, usually under the subheading of "Beyond the Basics."

Organization

This book is organized into sections. The first sections are learning steppingstones that take you to actual assembly. Following the assembly stage, the remaining sections tell you how to operate your computer.

To illustrate text, computer-generated representations are used in preference to photographs which sometimes tend to obscure clarity because of component crowding and shadow effects. These illustrations are consecutively titled as figures, with the first of a two-digit number separated by a hyphen being the section number. For increased clarity when a figure represents a major component such as the main system board, many of the subcomponents not under discussion are omitted. In order to facilitate quick reference during assembly, a list of illustrations is provided following the table of contents. The book also contains tables of information which are consecutively numbered as tables and also are included in the list of illustrations.

In some chapters, when "hands on" instructions are given, all keyboard type commands are shown in bold characters. Because the word *Enter* is used frequently, the notation <**Enter**> is used for "press Enter" or "pressing Enter."

Knowledge Levels

As with all "how to" books, the degree of ease with which the reader is able to create the subject of the book—in this case a computer—will largely depend upon previous familiarity with the subject or associated subjects. There is nothing mysterious about a PC, and building one involves the relatively simple process of assembling a number of components in a logical order and connecting cables at the right place. Nevertheless, acclimatization is provided in the sections preceding actual assembly by giving the reader a closer look at the PC, its components, and its cables.

This book offers adequate instruction for the average reader to assemble a computer from the basic parts. However, since the least easy stages of assembly are the ones involving the preparation and installation of the motherboard (main board, or system board), some readers may prefer to opt for the easier procedure described in the following paragraph.

"Bare Bones" Systems

At a relatively small extra cost over what would be charged for the individual components, what is known as a "bare bones" system can sometimes be ordered. This is a computer case which has been preassembled with power supply, motherboard, control panel, and control panel connections. For the reader who is hesitant to "plunge in at the deep end," taking this step will ensure completion of the project with relative ease, leaving only the memory, drives, and adapter cards to be installed.

Computers as a Way of Life

We hope the reader enjoys tackling this project and that those new to computers will be able to step into the computer age to benefit from the many advantages available to the intelligent user. Computers are a way of life as we head towards the twenty-first century, and as the Information Superhighway (or Internet) grows in strength, more and more information will become available—literally at your fingertips. If one is to be sure of finding a place in tomorrow's high-tech world, now is the time to start.

The computer is a tool which can be used to improve all areas within a working environment. It can be used to exploit opportunity and then to track profitability. Used properly, the computer can be a dollar maker—and that is what we hope yours will be.

Section 2

Overview

Types of Computers

There are three principal categories of business computer: the mainframe, the minicomputer, and the microcomputer (or personal computer). All serve the same basic function, which is to process information.

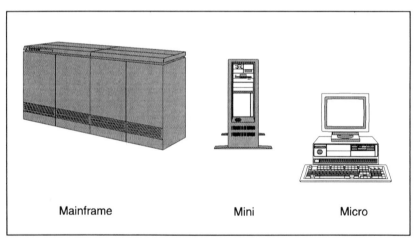

Mainframe   Mini   Micro

Figure 2-1   Types of computers

The forerunners of today's mainframes, the first true business computers were very large, slow machines using vacuum tubes instead of modern transistors, and they served a relatively small number of terminals. Most modern mainframe computers are much smaller (being in the large, lateral filing cabinet size range), much faster, and capable of serving a great number of terminals. Mainframe computers are usually found in large organizations: corporate, government, military, and research.

Minicomputers (minis) are about the height of a vertical two-drawer filing cabinet, but slimmer, and they also serve many terminals. They are usually found in smaller organizations that handle a substantial quantity of paperwork.

The principal function of mainframes and minis is to process and store data entered at cable-connected terminals. The terminals themselves have no capability to process or store data—they are "dumb" terminals.

Mainframes and minis preceded the microcomputer, although the stage was set for the micro when Bell Laboratories invented the transistor as a replacement for the vacuum tube soon after World War II. Ten years later, when Texas Instruments discovered how to make an integrated circuit containing several transistors, the way was open for the design of a microprocessor, or Central Processing Unit (CPU). Intel was first in the field with its 1-bit memory chip, then in 1972 Intel came out with a 4-bit CPU which was the catalyst for the commencement of microcomputer development. One great benefit of the 4-bit processor was its ability to move forward four bits of information in parallel, as opposed to in-line. To understand this better, consider the time taken for four people in line to pass a check point, compared with four people in line abreast—parallel. This principle continues to apply, and today's 16-bit processor is four times as fast as a 4-bit without consideration of any other modern technological advantages. Less than ten years after Intel's hesitant beginnings, IBM finalized and marketed its first serious contender in the microcomputer marketplace: the Personal Computer (PC). The PCs were slow stand-alones with no effective storage capacity, but they were relatively low priced and therefore attractive to personal users and small businesses. Several other makes (Apple, Altos, Commodore, etc.) made their appearance around this time, each with its own claim to fame and each with its own unique operating system. These days, the term PC (as a simple abbreviation for personal computer) is commonly used to describe virtually all desktop computers.

It transpired that IBM's patents were inadequate, allowing others to copy (clone) the IBM design, and as a result the term IBM-compatible came into being. Even the better-known brands such as Compaq, Epson, Kapro, and Tandy were originally clones of the IBM.

In the intervening years, PCs have been developed to the point where in speed and storage capacity they equal minis and even many mainframes. Further, through the use of networking software, they can be linked to work with other PCs or to act in the same way as a mainframe or mini by serving terminals. When the latest PCs are used to serve a network, they become a cost effective alternative to minis and some mainframes.

Beyond the Basics As with other computer companies, IBM had always referred to its computing devices as "systems," but the PC was unlike anything they had ever produced before; it was a "computer" and this is how they classed it. Because of IBM's choice of terminology there was a tendency in the field of information management to look at IBM's new Personal Computer as little more than an advanced calculator/typewriter, certainly not in the same class as the powerful mainframe computing systems they were accustomed to using.

The original PC had a mere 25K (kilobyte) of accessible memory (as compared with 16,000K commonly found in today's PC), and was limited to single-sided, single-density, 10K diskettes; thus there appeared to be some justification in the opinion, from an information management standpoint, of the PC being little more than a glorified typewriter. But there was a major difference. The PC boasted "system architecture," the creative integration of hardware and software but now uniquely housed in one small case. And without doubt the design was basically sound, for there are still some original PCs in use, albeit with improved memory, mass storage, and display, but still with the original system board. The critics were wrong: the PC was a system.

Comparing the original PC with today's version is akin to comparing the Wright brothers' flying machine with the supersonic Concorde jetliner. In both cases the original principles hold good, but both have been advanced almost immeasurably. Today's PC, with the speed and processing power of minicomputers and mainframes is, contrary to the early critics, very much a "system" with its own subsystems. These subsystems, with their own microprocessors, are the keyboard controller, a programmable interrupt controller to handle CPU requests, a direct memory access controller for the system memory, and others. The fact is, the PC embraces similar system specifics as mainframe computers.

Identifying a Suitable System Configuration

The Basic Computer

Speed of operation is the main variable in differing models, and increased speed will mean increased expenditure. The criteria that determines speed choice should be directly related to the application software programs to be used, but all too often the single criterion of capital outlay becomes the determining factor. If the application is to be no more complex than a basic word processing program, then speed of operation is not as significant as it would be for such applications as DTP (desktop publishing), CAD (computer aided design), or multimedia (combined usage of text, graphics, audio, animation, and full-motion).

However, although speed and application programs are the main considerations, product life as it relates to resale value and other factors should also be considered. As with most electronic equipment, there are advantages in owning the most recent computer technology; thus the 486 or Pentium family of computers (see **CPU** in Section 3) becomes a worthwhile choice.

The Monitor

Choices must be made regarding the quality and size of the monitor. Once again, if word processing is the only application, a small monochrome monitor is adequate, but if DTP, CAD, graphic-intensive programs, or multiwindowing are to be used, then a large screen displaying high-resolution color will be desirable. However, size, resolution, and color are functions of price; therefore, economics may again affect choice.

The Hard Disk Drive

Yet other considerations are hard disk drive size and speed. It used to be that a 20MB hard disk was adequate for storing the files of a simple word processing program, together with working files holding over a million and a half pages. Although one character still equals one byte, and 20,000,0000 characters, or 2,000,000 average sized words, still only require 20 MBs (megabytes), today's word processing application programs are so complex that the programs themselves use substantial disk space. For example, Microsoft Word 6.0 when fully installed requires 23MBs, and even a limited installation can call for

10MBs. Furthermore, owing to the immense popularity of Microsoft Windows, many popular PC applications have been written to run under Windows, thereby making the program almost a necessity. Microsoft Windows 3.11 needs over 10MBs, and if you install its subapplications such as Equation Editor, Note-It, WordArt, and others, another 8MBs can be absorbed. Graphic-intensive pages such as those generated by DTP and CAD applications average about ten times as many bytes as do text pages, and the programs themselves need anything from 10MBs to 30MBs of storage. Finally, if you plan on building a multimedia system, you will be looking for even more storage space. Consider as an absolute minimum a hard disk in the order of 60MBs, but be prepared to go to 200MBs or even more.

The speed at which information can be retrieved from a hard disk drive varies between makes and models. Quite recently, a speed of +/- 60ms (milliseconds) was the norm and was adequate for word processing, while +/- 15ms was adequate for DTP and CAD. However, today, even 20ms is not considered to be especially fast, and most hard disk drives run between 8ms and 16ms.

As a result of the latest miniaturization technology, PC hard disk drives are now available with storage space measured in gigabytes (1,000 MBs). This technology has also brought prices tumbling down; for example, a good price for a 40MB drive a few years ago was $200. Today, the same money buys a 400MB drive.

The Printer

In most cases a computer is of little value without a printer and, yet again, price relates directly to the quality of such features as print resolution, speed, versatility, and noise level. For run-of-the-mill work, a low-cost, 9-wire dot matrix printer is satisfactory, but if high quality is required for correspondence, a 24-wire dot matrix printer becomes desirable. Even better would be a personal-style laser printer which has come into contention because of its ever-decreasing price. For camera-ready work as produced by DTP applications, a higher resolution laser printer is desirable, but prices spiral steadily upwards with improvement in resolution, especially for color. Ink- and bubble-jet printers fit somewhere in between dot-matrix and laser, in both output quality and price. For CAD work, a plotter is normally used. Plotters have pen-holding devices that move over sheets of drawing paper, following the lines and shapes produced on the monitor screen by CAD application programs.

The Modem and the Internet

The word *modem* is an acronym for modulator/demodulator. A modem communicates via the telephone system with similarly equipped computers elsewhere by converting digital computer voltage to analog telephone voltage. A few years ago, an average price for an external modem was $150; today, for the same specification, the average is closer to $60. A low-cost internal modem can be bought for as little as $15 and a low-cost internal fax/modem for $30. Better quality modems come with a software program that allows you to set up parameters and procedures. You then record modem phone numbers you plan to call, making communication no more complex than highlighting a number on the screen, pressing the Enter key, and then following instructions. Once the connection is made, the caller can access programs on the other computer with the caller's screen reflecting what is on the other screen.

A modem gives access to a vast range of services worldwide, from bulletin boards providing information such as the Dow to making transactions with your bank, all via the Information Superhighway, or Internet, which is the name now generally used. The basis of the Internet is the world-wide telephone system. Over recent years, organizations that have huge amounts of non-secret data and would like access to huge amounts of other data started to band together by setting up sophisticated versions of the bulletin boards computer "hackers" have been using for years, and this was the start of the Net. Anyone who has a computer fitted with a modem can leave it running and publicize the modem phone number, making all data on the hard disk available to anybody who calls the number through his own modem. Internet comprises many large organizations and very many small ones, each with its own bulletin board, but with growth came control. Now, it is necessary to have a form of password before you can delve into an organization's hard disk, and to get that password you must pay companies that control entry to the Net; think of them as toll roads.

The subject of the Internet is beyond the scope of this book; however, since most readers will want to access it, the Yellow Pages under Computer Bulletin Boards provides names of local companies that supply access to the Internet. The following is a list of national access organizations that also provide their own extensive services.

- America Online (800) 827-6364 ($9.95+ per month)
- CompuServe Information Service (800) 848-8199 ($8.95+ per month)
- Prodigy (800) 776-3449 ($14.95+ per month)
- Delphi Internet Services (800) 695-4005 ($10.00+ per month)
- Dow Jones News/Retrieval (800) 522-3567 ($1.50 per 1,000 characters downloaded)
- GEnie (301) 251-6475 ($8.95+ per month)
- Ziff-Davis Interchange (617) 252-5000 ($10.00+ per month)

Access providers' services vary, and you should obtain a full packet of information from them before making a choice. With usage limited to a couple of hours a day, your total costs (at the time this book was written) should not exceed $30 per month, but there is every indication costs will rise dramatically as the Net attracts more and more users who will clog up existing phones lines as they chase bits of information back and forth, culminating in the need for new and costly communication lines.

Section 3

The IBM-Compatible PC

Introduction

When Intel produced its 80286 CPU, IBM used it in a new model they described as a PC-AT (Advanced Technologies). By the time the 80386 CPU was introduced, IBM was marketing their new models with micro-channel architecture (described in the motherboard part of this section) so that there never was a true-blue PC-AT with a 386 board. However, there were IBM-compatible ATs into which 80386 CPUs could be installed. As a result, IBM-compatible AT-286 machines were developed, followed by IBM-compatible AT-386s, AT-486s, and the Pentium. Whereas the 80286 was once considered advanced technology, it is to all intents and purposes today, dead technology. With current pricing as low as it is, and with the demands of modern software applications for processing power, no new PCs are being built with an 80286 CPU, and the 80386 is following the same fate. We are, therefore, primarily concerned with the 80486, although if a reader wishes to build an 80386, there will be no meaningful difference in the assembly procedure.

Operating System

Although this section deals primarily with hardware, until software is introduced a personal computer has no operational value, and the first requirement is an operating system: a program which when loaded into RAM directs the PC to function along defined lines. The operating system used by IBM-compatible PCs has traditionally been DOS, which means, literally, Disk Operating System. However, there are other operating systems such as the proprietary one used by Apple-

Macintosh computers, and UNIX, first written for minis. In all cases, it is the operating system that allows and controls the flow of data to and from input and output devices; that is, data from the keyboard to RAM then to the monitor screen, from the screen back to RAM then to the hard disk drive, or from the screen or the hard disk back to RAM then to the printer. The operating system also allows disks to be formatted, files and directories to be created, disks to be checked, etc. New on the scene is Microsoft Windows 95, in simplicity an operating system implanted in Windows giving total compatibility with DOS, as well as providing enhanced Windows capability. However, because not all readers will necessarily wish to invest in Windows 95, this book will assume DOS to be the operating system of choice.

The Basics of Operation

Like all computers, the PC operates on the binary system ("bi" meaning "two") and the two are "on" and "off." In other words, the basis of a CPU is an ultra-high-speed switch that makes and breaks an electrical circuit. Each switching action is called a bit, with ON represented by 1 and OFF by 0. Using an 8-bit process, characters can be represented by a series of eight bits. For example, when the D key is pressed on the keyboard, the CPU is switched on and off eight times in the sequence shown in Figure 3-1 that follows. Other circuitry is then able to convert the signals either to a video representation which can be seen on the screen or to printer language for hard copy reproduction. The eight bits of a character make up one "byte."

Character	Binary Representation
D	0 1 0 0 0 1 0 0
O	0 1 0 0 1 1 1 1
S	0 1 0 1 0 0 1 1

Figure 3-1 Binary system

For those readers who are familiar with DOS but would like more knowledge, a subsection titled "An In-depth Look at DOS" appears at the end of this section.

Under the Cover

With the cover of a PC removed, the principal components are easily identified: they are the motherboard, the power supply, the adapter cards, the floppy disk drives, the hard disk drives, and the cabling.

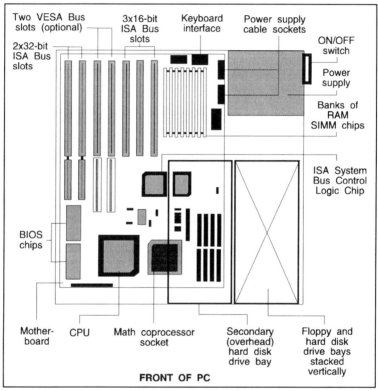

Figure 3-2   Principal components of a 486 desktop PC

Motherboard

The motherboard, which may be multilayered (as may other types of circuit boards and cards), incorporates printed circuits that link together all the electronic components such as transistors, memory chips, connectors, etc., that are located on the board. The connectors, properly known as expansion slots, accept adapter cards (or interface boards). The slots are connected to a parallel bus (in electrical parlance, bus means a rigid connector that can accept a number of electrical circuits). In a PC, the bus is usually ISA (Industry Standard Architecture), although the EISA bus is available on some models (see "Beyond the Basics" below). A relatively old technique, called local-bus, has recently been refined by a group of companies working in conjunction with VESA (Video Electronics Standards Association). The product is called VL-Bus, or simply VESA and is also covered in "Beyond the Basics" below.

Until recently, the adapter cards for both IBM and IBM-compatible PCs measured four inches in height and slotted into an ISA bus as shown in Figure 3-3. Later IBM models, called PS/2, accepted much smaller cards and the rigid connector is known as "micro-channel" or "micro-bus."

This book deals with the 16-bit and 32-bit ISA bus.

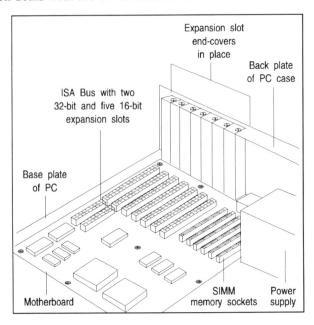

Figure 3-3 Example of an ISA bus

Beyond the Basics When IBM took steps to regain its position in the PC marketplace following the enormous growth in sales of clones, it abandoned its original architecture—Industry Standard Architecture (ISA)—and created its heavily patented Micro Channel Architecture (MCA) which, as well as reducing the height available for adapter cards, provided greatly improved functionality. This latter feature, together with the strength of IBM's name, won the hearts of corporate America, and sales by clone manufacturers declined, as did sales by adapter card manufacturers because of the height problem. Not to be outdone, a group of nine major manufacturers developed the Extended Industry Standard Architecture (EISA), which has most of the improved functions found in the MCA but with the one big advantage of retaining compatibility with the billions of dollars of existing ISA hardware; thus the clone business thrived again. Faced with the inevitable, IBM quietly killed off its PS/2 series with its micro-channel architecture, leaving corporate America with a lot of obsolete machines.

Modern CPUs operate at speeds generally in excess of 25MHz (for an understanding of MHz, see "Beyond the Basics" following the subsection "CPU," below), yet must be compatible with old CPUs operating at speeds as low as 8MHz. Compatibility is necessary to enable hardware and software originally designed to function with 8MHz CPUs to function on the faster units. To do this, the ISA system bus control logic (see Figure 3-2) in a fast CPU slows instructions down to 8MHz and limits them to a 16-bit data path. The outcome of this, regardless of what hardware and software is in use, is to create a data-bottleneck which can slow down activities such as screen redraw time, particularly with high-resolution monitors capable of millions of colors. You can overcome this problem by using a motherboard fitted with a local bus such as VL-Bus. A local bus is able to bypass the ISA system bus control logic chip, allowing instructions to travel on the 32-bit CPU bus and the 32-bit data path at speeds up to 40MHz.

Chips

A "chip" is an electronic module with its own micro-printed circuitry, varying in size from that of a button on a small calculator to the shift key on a computer keyboard.

BIOS

The BIOS (Basic Input/Output System) chips (usually two, but sometimes one) contain the preprogrammed instructions that make the PC active after turning on (known as powering up or "booting," although booting more accurately refers to the stage when DOS takes over from the BIOS).

CMOS

A CMOS (Complimentary Metal Oxide Semiconductor) memory chip is user-programmed to store the system configuration, such as time and date, amount of memory, disk drive configuration, and monitor specification, but for this information to be retained when the PC is not in use it is backed up by a small internal battery.

CPU

The most important chip is the CPU, or microprocessor, the heart of the system once it has been turned on. This chip interprets and routes the information that is fed into the PC. Information (instructions) can be input from a keyboard, a mouse, a digitizing tablet, a modem, a scanner, or a floppy disk, and even by voice on a system appropriately configured.

Although Intel has traditionally enjoyed the greatest sales of CPU chips, other makes have recently appeared in the marketplace resulting in more competitive pricing, making very fast 486 CPUs affordable alternatives to slower versions and to 386 CPUs. A 386 CPU has a computing performance index relative to the original PC ranging from 15 to 40, whereas a fast 486 CPU is in the order of 80. Nevertheless, the top spot goes to Intel's Pentium, and although at this point in time it is rather expensive, it is twice as fast as a 486. An interesting CPU statistic is that the Pentium CPU contains over 3 million transistors; almost three times as many as a 486 CPU.

Beyond the Basics   The architecture of a CPU determines the speed rating, the size of the data bus, and the size of the address bus which, in turn, dictates the computer's memory capacity.

CPU speed is measured in megahertz (MHz), previously described as CPS (cycles per second) but subsequently changed in honor of Heinrich Rudolph Hertz for his experimental work in electro-magnetism during the late nineteenth century. Thus, a CPU with a clock speed of 25MHz is completing 25 million cycles per second and, depending on the efficiency of the CPU, using perhaps 5 cycles to execute a single instruction (i.e., one step in a batch of steps that instructs the computer to carry out a task). Because of the varying efficiency of CPUs, the measure of cycles per second does not give a true indication of processing speed; thus the term MIPS (millions of instructions per second) is now commonly used. Taking the above figures of 25MHz and 5-cycle efficiency, the computer would be rated at 5.0 MIPS.

The Intel 8088 CPU chosen for the original IBM PC, and most of its clones, had an 8-bit data path: to all intents and purposes an 8-wire path along which eight bits can travel in parallel, which results in the movement of one full byte at a time (see "The Basics of Operation" and Figure 3-1 in this section). The eight paths represent width; therefore, the CPU is said to have an 8-bit bus. The Intel 80286 CPU has a 16-bit bus which permits the movement of two bytes at a time, significantly speeding up processing time. Because of the reasons described in the next paragraph, the 80386SX CPU also has a 16-bit bus, but the 80386DX and subsequent DX CPUs have the 32-bit bus; however, at this time there are relatively few adapter cards available that can take advantage of the 32-bit bus.

The internal architecture of SX CPUs is less complicated than that of the DX, thereby permitting lower production costs. However, you cannot rob Peter without paying Paul, and while the architecture allows 32-bit processing within the system, it restricts communication out of the system to 16 bits.

The address bus is distinctly different from the data bus, being the width of the wire path that carries addressing information to specify a location for data in the memory. Each wire carries a single bit of information that is a single digit in the address, and because a computer works on the binary numbering principle, a 2-bit bus would provide only four addresses (00, 01, 10, and 11), and a 3-bit bus eight addresses (000, 001, 010, 011, 100, 101, 110, 111). The 8088 CPU which had a 20-bit address bus provided for 1,048,576 addresses—the equivalent of a megabyte—thus the maximum memory addressable by the 8088 CPU was 1MB. The 80286 CPU has a 24-bit address bus providing 16,777,216 addresses and, therefore, is able to address 16MB of memory, while all 80386 and 80486 DX CPUs with their 32-bit address bus provide 4,294,967,296 addresses and could handle 4,096MB although, of course, sockets are not provided for anything like this amount of memory.

Table 3-1 that follows lists Intel CPUs, from its 8088 used in IBM's early PC to its latest Pentium.

Table 3-1   Intel CPU specifications

Model	Max Speed (MHz)	Internal Data Bus (In Bits)	External Data Path (In Bits)	Addres-sable Memory (MB)	Number of Trans-istors
8088	8	16	8	1	29,000
8086	8	16	16	1	29,000
80C86	8	16	16	1	29,000
80186	16	16	16	1	35,000
80286	20	16	16	16	130,000
80386SX	33	32	16	16	275,000
80386DX	40	32	32	4096	275,000
80486SX	40	32	16	16	900,000
80486DX	50	32	32	4096	1.2M
80486DX2	66	32	32	4096	1.2M
80486DX4	100	32	32	4096	1.2M
Pentium	90	32	64	4096	3.1M

The DX2 series of CPU refers to a basic DX with a form of overdrive that doubles its clock speed. DX2s have two clock speeds: 50MHz (25 doubled) and 66MHz (33 doubled). The DX4 series is a basic 33.3MHzDX with clock speed tripled to 100MHz but is slower than a Pentium.

The Pentium CPU offers the following advantages over the 80486:

- At least twice as fast as a 486
- Supports a 32-bit instruction set
- Built-in coprocessor
- Built-in cache
- Ability to process two instructions per clock cycle

The Pentium disadvantages are:

- Price
- Heat (a special heat-sink with fan is recommended)
- Few available software applications can take advantage of the CPU's 64-bit external data path

Memory Chips

Of the many other chips that assist in processing, analyzing, filtering, and routing the computer's two-way flow of information, the best known are likely to be the memory chips.

Memory chips provide the computer with Random Accessible Memory (RAM): a volatile memory that only becomes active when the computer is turned on (or booted), and disappears like mist evaporating when the computer is turned off (referred to as powering down).

Information you input is held in RAM and must be transferred to a storage disk before the computer powers down, otherwise it will be totally lost.

A few years ago, only DIP (Dual Inline Package) RAM chips were available. They were individual chips that plugged directly into the main board in banks of nine. You may come across DIP chips in older model PCs, and Figure 3-4 is included only for sake of interest. DIP chips came in memory sizes of 64K, 256K, or 1MB, and nine chips were required to provide an equivalent amount of memory.

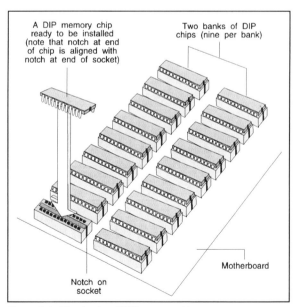

Figure 3-4   Two banks of DIP memory chips

The standard memory to be found in today's PC is SIMM (Single Inline Memory Module), usually in banks of three or nine miniaturized chips on mini-cards with either a 30-pin or 72-pin strip connector. SIMM modules plug into sockets on the main board. Figure 3-5 shows a 1MB SIMM module and socket. SIMM memory modules are available in 256K, 1MB, 4MB, 8MB, 16MB, and 32MB sizes.

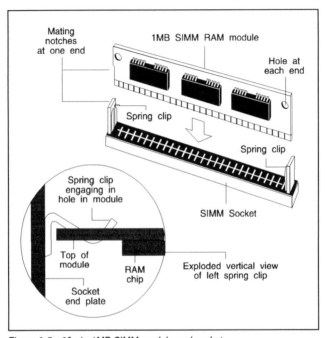

Figure 3-5   30-pin 1MB SIMM module and socket

Two other types of memory chip are S-RAM and D-RAM, similar in design to a DIP RAM memory chip, and used respectively as RAM cache and video memory. (See "Beyond the Basics" that follows.)

Beyond the Basics

RAM   Technological advances made in recent years in the production of low-cost, miniaturized memory devices are one of the prime reasons for the high speed, flexibility, and popularity of today's PC.

Most machines today are delivered with at least 4MB of memory which, as a point of interest, is in line with what mainframes used over a decade ago to serve hundreds of terminals.

The PC uses RAM for temporary program instruction storage and data storage. The great advantage of computer memory as compared with a recording tape is the "random" feature. The contents of each storage cell can be directly accessed through the chip connector pins, whereas a tape must be moved forward or back to the part containing the information to be recovered.

Two of the several attributes of a memory chip are capacity and speed. Capacity is specified in kilobytes or megabytes and speed in nanoseconds. Speed relates to the time required by a chip to accept an instruction following receipt of the previous one; therefore, the lower the nanosecond rating, the faster the chip. Chip speed will directly influence system performance; however, because most SIMM chips sold today have speeds of 60ns or 70ns, differences in performance will not usually be readily discernible. It used to be that when slow chips (above 100ns) were used in 60286 machines, there would be a delay in processor activity because of the time lapses between acceptance of instructions by the memory. This delay in processor activity is called a wait-state, and the number of wait-states needed to match memory chip speed was set by jumpered switches. Wait-states are mentioned here only out of general interest.

One of the chips, or a cell in a chip, in a SIMM module is a controller that keeps track of the total memory. Memory can become corrupted from a number of causes and, when discovered by the controller chip, or cell, the processor is advised through an interrupt called the non-maskable interrupt. An interrupt is no more than a temporary suspension of processor activity, but in most cases of memory problems the suspension becomes permanent and the system must be powered down and restarted after the fault has been corrected.

Cache Memory   The RAM cache is a technique used to speed up data flow between main memory and the CPU. Chips similar in appearance to DIP provide RAM for the cache, but at the ultra-high speed of 20ns. Cache RAM is very expensive. The RAM cache is built into the motherboard or the CPU and is used to temporarily store data or software code currently in use. When you, or your software application, make a request to the CPU, the cache intercepts the request, and if the requested information is in the cache, it is delivered to the CPU, obviating the necessity for the CPU to search for the information on the hard disk. As the cache assembles data, it develops an algorithm which is able to anticipate the needs of the CPU, thereby further speeding up the computing process.

Video Memory Although 128K of conventional memory (as described in the subsection that follows) is allotted for video use, monitors displaying high-resolution and many colors require more memory in order to refresh the screen at a speed not apparent to the viewer. The higher the resolution and the greater the number of colors, the more demand for memory increases. Multimedia in particular not only demands great processing power but also very fast memory.

Types and Modes of Memory There are three types of memory— conventional, expanded, and extended—and three memory modes— real, protected, and 386 enhanced. Conventional memory consists of the first megabyte, of which 640K is the base memory for user programs and data, 128K is for on-screen display of text and graphics, another 128K is ROM (read only memory) for the use of adapter cards, and a final 128K is for ROM in the system BIOS. Until version 5.0 of DOS became available, the system (and therefore the user) was only able to work with the first 640K. DOS 5.0 and later versions are able to work with portions of upper memory which can result in freeing up more base memory for application software programs. When restricted to the first 640K, the computer is in the "real mode." Figure 3-6 portrays memory maps for CPUs prior to and after the 80286.

The term "real mode" came into being when the 80286 CPU was designed and, in order to allow for compatibility, an 8088 mode (real mode) was built in. However, compatibility was obliged to be 100% and, as a result, the new 286 CPU merely operated like a very fast XT, with no other benefits and no way to make use of memory above one megabyte.

As application programs became larger, needing more memory, efforts were made to solve the problem by Lotus, Intel, and Microsoft. The three computer companies developed a technique known as bank switching which increases the apparent address space without increasing the number of hardware address lines and made possible the use of expanded memory. Expanded memory used a fixed block of address space in the first megabyte of memory to serve as a window onto a much larger array of memory which does not have an address in the 8088 memory map. This technique became known as the Lotus-Intel-Microsoft Expanded Memory Specification (LIM EMS) and it enabled software programs that recognized it to draw on memory above one megabyte a page at a time. The original EMS specification provided up to 8MB of bank switchable memory, but this was revised in version 4.0 of the EMS to provide a maximum of 32 megabytes.

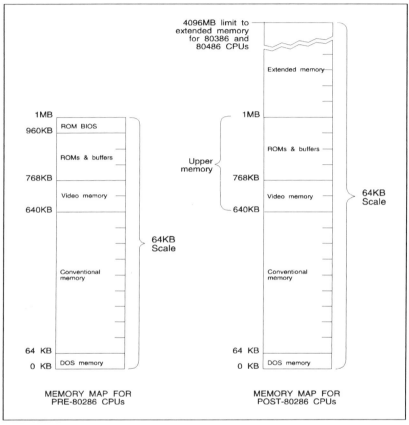

Figure 3-6 Memory maps

Fortunately, users were not stuck for too long with this useful but somewhat cumbersome technique. With the advent of Windows 3.0 (and other software), memory above the first megabyte became accessible as extended memory when the 80286 processor was running in its natural mode, the Virtual Protected Mode.

The 386 enhanced mode, which includes the 386SX and up, can be used with appropriate software to create virtual memory by using a free portion of the hard disk. Virtual memory must be recreated each time a computer is turned on.

Power Supply

The power supply converts standard 115-volt 60Hz AC current to a 5-volt DC current acceptable to the microcircuits and components of a computer, and to a 12-volt DC current for the motors driving the fan and the disk drives.

Power supply failures are not uncommon in PCs, and it is generally better to over-power so far as wattage is concerned. Old PCs used 150W and 200W power supplies; today's PCs use a 200W or better supply.

The fan that the power supply drives to cool the computer may become ineffective in excessive ambient temperatures; for this reason the computer should be housed in a suitable environment. Because the fan draws cooling air into the computer, the environment should also be free of dust and pollution.

The power supply in the PC itself has a connection to a regular power supply, but this should be via a surge protector to protect the delicate electronic circuitry and chips against current fluctuations which, at the least, might garble data or, at the worst, burn out electronic units, losing all data. Better than a surge protector is an Uninterruptible Power Supply (UPS) which contains a battery capable of running the system for about 10 minutes so that the operator can save data and power down in an orderly manner in the event of a power outage.

Adapter Cards

An adapter (interface) card is a printed circuit board fitted with chips and other components. An adapter card may be multi-layered. For cards serving external peripherals, one end will be fitted with a connector (called a port) designed to accept a cable from the peripheral device. The card installs into an expansion slot on the main board, with the connector end exposed through a slot at the back of the computer as shown in Figure 3-7. For a computer to operate it must have two adapter cards: a video adapter card for connection to a monitor and a drive controller for connection to floppy and hard disk drives (although in some designs, the display and disk drive circuits of these cards are built into the motherboard, eliminating the need for separate cards).

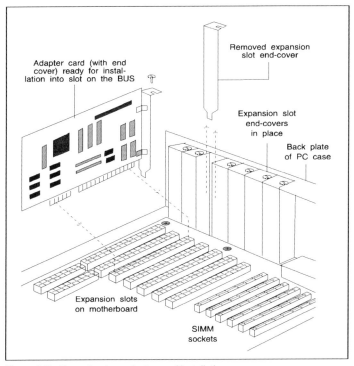

Figure 3-7   Example of an adapter card installation

Adapter cards are also needed for:

- Bus-mouse
- Disk drives (hard and floppy)
- External serial devices (modems, printers, and mice)
- Extra printer ports
- Internal modems
- Joy sticks
- Mainframe connections
- Networking
- Plotters
- Printers
- Scanners
- Speed
- Sound
- Video

Surprisingly, adapter cards are seldom identified with a printed name, and it is necessary to learn how to distinguish one from another. Generally, recognition is by the type of interface. For example, a bus-mouse card has a port (plug) which is unique to the connector at the end of the mouse cable, a disk controller card has rows of exposed pins that match the connector on the ribbon cable, an internal modem card has a phone socket, etc.

Floppy Disk Drives

A floppy disk drive is a device with a magnetic head that can write and/or read information to and from a floppy disk. At one time, PCs were limited to a drive that accepted a 5.25-inch disk with maximum storage capacity of 360K, and later with 3.5-inch disks of 720K capacity. (For the convenience of quick mental math, we say that 1K equals 1,000 bytes, although in fact it equals 1,024 bytes.) 80286 through 80486 machines are installed with 5.25- or 3.5-inch drives for disks of 1.2MB and 1.44 respectively, or 3.5-inch/2.88MB providing MS-DOS v5.0 or better is installed. The tendency is for fewer 5.25-inch drives to be installed in new machines, largely because most new software applications are supplied on 3.5-inch disks, because the 3.5-inch disk has greater storage capacity, and because it is more durable.

Floppy disks are inserted in an exposed slot at the front of the drive which is designated A if there is only one drive, or A and B if there are two which is the maximum.

Beyond the Basics Most times, a new disk drive is properly configured and care need only be taken to ensure that the ribbon cable is properly connected. However, disk drives have configuration devices, of which the main ones are:

- Drive-select jumper
- Terminating resistor

Drive-select Jumper A disk controller card and the system's drive subsystem recognize a drive by a unique single-digit number, with numbers commencing at 0. (This is not to be confused with the DOS method of recognizing a drive by a single letter commencing with A.) The default jumper setting is for drive 0. For further information consult the manual supplied with the drive.

Terminating Resistor Most of the ribbon cables that connect a drive to the controller have two drive connectors, allowing two drives to be connected via one cable to the controller. The drive connected from the end of the cable must always have its terminating resistor in place, even if it is the only drive. In the case of a second drive connected from within the length of the cable, the terminating resistor must be removed.

Floppy Disks

The 5.25-inch disk   This disk and the jacket in which it resides are flexible. The disk in its jacket is normally stored in an open-ended envelope. The capacity is generally indicated on the brand label with "DD" for 360K, and "HD" for 1.2MB. A section of the magnetic disk is exposed through an opening at one end (the end that is placed first into the computer or into the envelope for storage) and this is where the drive "reads" the disk. Exposed areas of any disk must not be touched. Labels are provided for titling disks but, when affixed to the disk, titling must be by soft felt-tip pen and not by pencil or ball-point pen, which may damage the media. Damage can also be caused by warping if disks are left in direct sunlight.

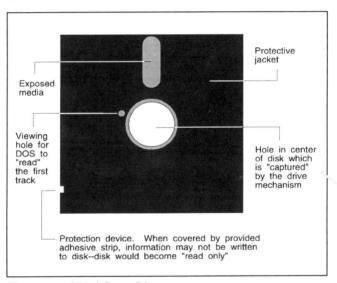

Figure 3-8   5.25-inch floppy disk

After inserting a disk into the drive—label up, and reading end in first—a lever must be turned to cause the drive to capture the disk. When the disk is in use, an activity warning light on the drive face will activate. When the disk is no longer needed for the application, it should be removed and safely stored.

The 3.5-inch disk   Although still referred to as a floppy disk, a semi-rigid plastic case permanently houses the flexible disk, and therefore it is more durable than the 5.25-inch. Capacity is indicated by "DD" for 720K, "HD" for 1.44MB, and "DM" (Dual Media) for

2.88MB. The area where the drive head reads the disk is covered by a spring-loaded metal cover that can be slid to one side—this is done mechanically when the disk is placed in the drive and should never be moved by hand. Labels are provided for titling, and because of the hard nature of the disk cover, most types of writing implements may be safely used. As with all electronic devices, care must be exercised in the handling of the disk, and it should not be left in direct sunlight.

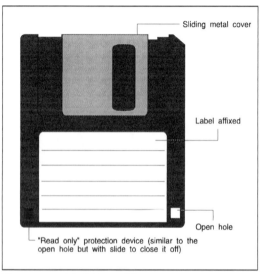

Figure 3-9   3.5-inch floppy disk

Beyond the Basics   The manufacturer's label on a 5.25-inch disk generally states that it is double-sided, double- or high-density, soft- or hard-sectored (avoid buying hard-sectored disks), and with 40 or 96 tracks per side (tracks are concentric, circular rings). Since a double-density disk invariably has 40 tracks per side, and a high-density disk 96, the track information is often omitted from the label. In fact, density describes both longitudinal and linear density, with the former referring to tracks per inch and the latter to the amount of data a track can store.

CD-ROM Drives

A CD-ROM drive may be installed as the B drive, but it is, of course, a read only drive. The advantage of CD-ROM is the immense storage capacity of the CD-ROM disk—up to 650MB; its disadvantage is its relatively slow transfer speed, although the newer quad-speed drives achieve data transfer rates in the order of 600 KBps (kilobytes per second). Until recently, CD-ROM drives used the SCSI interface which often proved difficult to install; now there are new drives appearing that use the simple-to-install IDE interface. (See *Interfaces* under "Beyond the Basics" in the "Hard Disk Drives" subsection below.)

Hard Disk Drives

Like floppy disk drives, hard disk drives also have magnetic heads to read or write data, but they do not usually have a removable disk. The disk is a series of vertical platters, each with its own magnetic head, with total capacity ranging into hundreds of megabytes. In addition to their great storage capacity, hard disk drives are able to transfer information bits very much faster than a floppy drive. Hard drives are not accessible from outside the computer but, like floppy drives, they have an indicator light that shows when the drive is in use. Like all electronic devices, hard disk drives can malfunction, and when they do there is a risk that stored data may be destroyed. Therefore, the stored information from hard discs should be copied (backed up) regularly onto floppy disks or tapes.

Care should be taken not to jar a disk drive (hard or floppy) by jolting a computer while it is in use, otherwise the magnetic head(s) that read and write data may strike the disk or platter, causing damage that may result in loss of data or even total destruction.

Modern hard disks have an auto-parking device that keeps the heads away from the platters when the computer is not in use. You should determine from your supplier if this feature is present on the hard disk you buy.

Before use, all disks must be formatted, and some hard disks, but specifically not ones with the IDE interface (see *Interfaces* below), must also be initialized before formatting. Formatting refers to procedures normally carried out using the disk operating system (DOS) software to organize a magnetic disk so that it is able to receive data in a specific format.

Beyond the Basics

Size Differing makes and models of hard disk drives result in a variety of physical sizes. There are 3.5-inch and 5.25-inch widths, and full- or half-heights. Height is largely determined by the number of vertically stacked platters, and the number of platters influence the total storage capacity of a hard disk, the other measurement of size. A half-height disk is most often used in a PC, and it measures about 1.5-inch in height. Installation of a 3.5-inch drive in computer cases with 5.25-inch drive bays requires an adapter kit in order for it to fit.

The platters of a hard disk store data on both sides on a number of tracks. Two tracks in corresponding positions on each side of the platters are called a cylinder.

Drive-select Jumpers   Modern hard disks have drive-select jumpers (but not terminating resistors) usually mounted on the drive's logic board. If two drives (which must be similar) are installed, the jumpers on the second must be reset.

Speed   Hard disks are considerably faster than floppy disks with speed being measured in two ways: access time and transfer rate. Access time is the average time taken for the reading heads to move from one cylinder to the next, while transfer rate is the speed that the drive can send data to the motherboard.

Interfaces   An interface matches the output of one device with the input of another device. Among the different types of controller/drive interfaces, or data encoding schemes, are MFM (Modified Frequency Modulation), RLL (Run Length Limited), ESDI (Enhanced Small Disk Interface), SCSI (Small Computer System Interface— pronounced "scuzzy"), and IDE (Integrated Drive Electronics). Most of today's drives use either the IDE or the SCSI interface, and it is recommended you use IDE. Advantages of the IDE interface are very low cost and the fact that the disk is pre-initialized (low-level formatted). You will realize that because of the sensitive inter-relationship between a drive and its controller it is essential for them to be properly matched.

Interleave Specifications   Each track on a platter is divided into sectors, much like the slices of a pie, with the sectors numbered consecutively upward from 1. As the platter spins at high speed, the head reads a sector and transmits the data to the motherboard and is then ready for the next sector. Unfortunately, 2 has passed, and the head must wait for all the other sectors (up to 17, or even 26) to pass before 2 comes round again. Interleaving renumbers sectors on a disk in an order selected to suit the transfer rate of the drive, so that the next sector due to be read is there when the head is ready. Drives formatted with a 1:1 interleave can transmit data at rates from 500 to 1,000 KBps (depending on the interface) as compared with 130 to 300 at a 4:1 interleave. Most modern hard disk drives have 1:1 interleaving.

Cables

There are several types of cable in a PC: six individually colored wires from the power supply to the main board; four individually colored wires from the power supply to the disk drives; ribbon cables from the disk controller adapter card to the disk drives; mini-ribbon cables between input/output (I/O) adapter cards and communication ports; and lightweight colored wires between the main board and external buttons and indicator lights on the control panel.

Peripherals

Basically, peripherals include any equipment not housed inside the computer and connected by some form of data transfer cable. Some peripherals may receive their operating electrical supply via the data cable, or they may have their own, separate power cable. Examples with connection information follow.

Keyboards

Information on types of keyboards is given at the end of Section 4. They use a spiral cable with a 5-pin connector that fits directly to the main board through a round port, most times at the back of the computer.

Mice and Joysticks

Used as alternatives to keyboards to input commands to the computer, these peripherals are connected by cable to a serial communications port, or in the case of a bus-mouse to a unique adapter card.

Monitors

There are probably more monitor makes and models than any other peripheral, so many in fact that to cover them adequately would call for a complete book. What follows is a summary of salient features.

> **Color or Monochrome** In nearly all cases of private ownership, price is the ruling factor. The resolution of a relatively

low-cost monochrome monitor is invariably better than the resolution of the cheapest color monitor, and even then the price difference is marked. If color is essential, for your eyes' sake, go for the highest resolution you can afford, but keep in mind that the video card also controls resolution. The most expensive color monitor will not provide high resolution if matched with a cheap video card.

Resolution If you view a black-and-white photograph reproduced in a newspaper through a magnifying glass, you will see it is made up of dots. Similarly, the display on a monitor screen is made from dots, described as picture elements (pixels). Resolution varies from a display on the screen of 640 x 200 pixels through 1600 x 1200 pixels. With color monitors, another way to define resolution is by dot pitch, which relates to the size of the dots of phosphor on the screen which are lit up. Dot pitch ranges from a low of about .50mm to a high of .25mm.

Connections Monitors use a shielded cable with a connector where the pin count varies according to the type of monitor. The connector interfaces to a port on the video card which projects through one of the slots at the back of the computer. (Simple monochrome video cards usually also have a printer port.)

Scanners

The modern scanner is available in hand-held models which roll over the media being scanned; desk models which accept 8.5-inch media through rollers; and flatbed models where the media is laid on a glass plate and a hinged cover is closed over it, like a copier. Scanners create a grayscale or color bitmapped image which can be brought to the monitor screen via a graphics or paint application program where it can be edited. By using special "optical character" reading programs, scanned text can be put into word processing programs for editing and printing. Scanners are connected by cable to a port on a scanner adapter card.

External Drives

Hard, CD-ROM, and floppy drives may be located externally in a special housing. They are connected by cable to a special disk drive controller card through a port at the back of the computer. This connection also provides the electrical power to operate the drive.

Printers

Like monitors, there are an immense number of printers on the market, but they define more easily into four types: dot-matrix printers, ink- or bubble-jet printers, laser printers, and color printers using various technology including ink-jet, hot-wax transfer, dye sublimation, and laser.

Dot-matrix printers Affordable printers with choices of resolution to allow for fast drafting or slower, near letter quality printing, and reasonably good quality graphics reproduction; some have color capability. These printers are noisy in operation, although new improved sound deadening designs have reduced sound emissions.

Ink- and bubble-jet printers An alternative when a laser is too expensive and dot-matrix resolution inadequate. These printers give resolutions up to 360 dpi (dots per inch) and more, they are silent and quite fast. Some jet printers use a water-based ink which is, therefore, not waterproof. Color versions are available at reasonable prices. Despite their relatively high resolution, character definition is usually not up to the standard of a laser printer owing to ink bleed.

Laser printers With resolutions ranging from 300 to 1,200 dpi, silent operation, together with speed and simplicity of use, the laser is a first choice if it can be afforded, and in the lower resolution range prices are not high.

Color printers Necessarily more expensive than grayscale printers, color printers have a place in the corporate environment. Presentations in color are often more effective than grayscale, particularly when differentiating detail on graphs and charts. Color printing is also a valuable tool for a desktop publisher to see a preview of what printshop output in color will look like.

Printers use a shielded serial cable or a parallel cable which may or may not be shielded. A parallel cable permits the flow of eight data bytes in line abreast, whereas in a serial cable the flow is one bit after another, therefore parallel data communication is faster and is preferred. The cable connector interfaces with a port on a monochrome video card; on a special printer card; or on a multifunction I/O card.

After connecting a printer cable to a printer port, you must identify the printer with any application programs you are running. Most applications ask for printer specification at the time the software is loaded, and they also make provision for the information to be provided when a printer is added later.

Plotters

The key features of a plotter is the size of media it can accept; speed and accuracy of operation; and the number of pens it can control. Media sizes range from 8.5-inch x 11-inch sheets through rolls of 36-inch width. Plotters usually have rollers which move the media backward and forward under the pen, while the pen itself moves laterally, thus high-speed movement in two directions allows even the finest detail to be plotted quite rapidly. Advanced plotters have automatic pen changers so that color can be varied on command from the computer. Connectivity is by shielded serial cable that interfaces to a serial port.

Modems

An internal modem resides on an adapter card which has a jack for a telephone line connection, accessible through one of the rear slots of the computer. An external modem connects by cable to a communications (serial) port at the back of the computer. The telephone line connection goes directly to a jack in the external modem.

The speed at which a modem can transmit data is called the baud rate. A modem with a rate of 1200 baud is transmitting data at roughly 1200 bits per second. A modem with a faster baud rate of 9600 is more desirable, but it should be borne in mind that if the modem you are calling is of a slower specification, data transmission will be at the rate of the slower modem. Many modern modems incorporate a FAX, enabling you to output incoming messages to your printer.

Networks

The connection between networked computers is by shielded coaxial cable or twisted-pair cable (telephone cable) interfaced to ports on the network adapter cards.

Mainframes

Connection to a mainframe is from a port on a card designed specially to interface with the mainframe. Often, this connection will be to a remote (out-of-building or out-of-town) mainframe and will be made by modem on a regular or dedicated telephone line.

An In-Depth Look at DOS

DOS means different things to different people. Some use it only as the means to execute the commands they type on the keyboard; others, who access their application programs via a shell with a menu or via Windows, seldom make use of DOS; and programmers use DOS as an interface to disk, directory, and file functions.

Loading DOS

When a PC is switched on, built-in routines prepare the system to accept DOS. First, details of the computer's BIOS (Basic Input/Output System) are displayed on the monitor and an opportunity is given the user to enter setup in order to alter the system settings stored in the BIOS chip. Next, the start-up routines look at drive A to see if DOS is waiting to be loaded. If DOS is not there, the BIOS looks for it on other installed drives. If DOS is not found, either a cursor blinks under the last displayed line on the monitor until DOS is provided, or a message is displayed asking for a DOS disk.

If a bootable hard disk (usually drive C) is not installed, a DOS boot disk must be inserted in drive A prior to booting so that when the BIOS looks at drive A it will find DOS, activate the disk drive, and read DOS into memory. If a hard disk containing DOS is installed, it is not necessary to insert a DOS boot disk, since the BIOS will pass over drive A and find DOS when it looks at drive C.

To help understand how DOS functions, visualize it loading in three separate stages as shown in Figure 3-10.

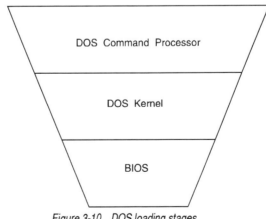

Figure 3-10 DOS loading stages

Every computer is supplied with the previously referred to set of routines programmed into the BIOS chip. Some routines are more elegant than others; the original PC routines were simplistic, while modern PCs can be complex, but each time you switch on your computer, the last action of the BIOS routine is to look for a boot record on a disk. The boot record is contained in the first sector of any bootable disk and, when found, it initiates the bootstrap program (hence the expression "booting a computer"). Incidentally, the object of the routines always looking at drive A first is to make it possible for you to boot from a floppy disk in the event of hard disk failure.

The bootstrap program makes use of the input/output routines found in the read only memory (ROM) of the BIOS chip, together with the hidden file IO.SYS to create a space in random accessible memory (RAM) to handle input and output. The file IO.SYS is one of two hidden files which are referred to in the display of information that follows execution of the DOS command CHKDSK (check disk). By communicating with the routines in ROM, DOS translates the information into a format the input/output devices are able to understand. With some devices such as mice and scanners, a DEVICE=nnn entry may be required in the CONFIG.SYS file, with "nnn" being the device name.

The DOS kernel, or program section as it is sometimes called, is created during the starting procedure by the file MSDOS.SYS (the other hidden file) which is read into memory. The kernel controls the functions shown in the following list.

- File management (create, delete, edit)
- Directory management (make, remove, alter)
- Writing (to screen, disk, or printer)

The command processor carries out your commands by using the file COMMAND.COM. Consisting of three sections named startup, transient, and resident, the command processor is the key to user control of your computer; without it you cannot function.

The startup section has the task of executing the commands in the AUTOEXEC.BAT file and, as soon as that procedure is finished, the startup section is removed in order to free memory for other usage.

The complete sequence from the beginning to the end of DOS startup is shown schematically in Figure 3-11.

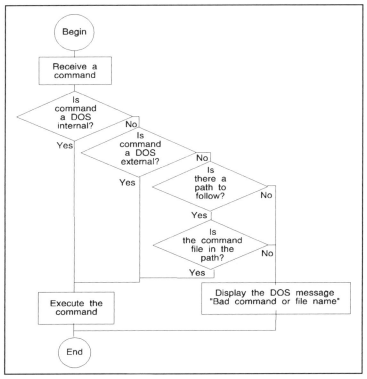

Figure 3-11   DOS startup stages

DOS After Startup

The transient section of DOS is so named because many application programs overwrite it, and when the application program is terminated the resident section, which is held in memory at all times, reloads the transient section; a vital action because the transient section holds all the DOS internal commands, which are given in Table 3-2 that follows.

Table 3-2   DOS internal commands

BREAK	DATE	PATH	TIME
CHDIR	DEL	PROMPT	TYPE
CLS	DIR	REN	VER
COPY	ERASE	RMDIR	VERIFY
CITY	MKDIR	SET	VOL

DOS external commands are those which are left in the DOS files on either the DOS floppy disk or your hard disk. When a DOS internal command is received, it is pulled from the transient section and executed. When a DOS external command is received, such as DISKCOPY, it is taken from the DISCOPY.EXE file providing that file is in root or its location is defined in a path statement (see next paragraph). Failure by DOS to find the file results in the message, "Bad command or file name." Figure 3-12 tracks the stages following a DOS command.

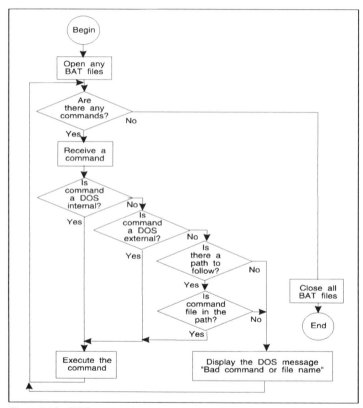

Figure 3-12   DOS command processor stages

A path statement is merely an instruction to DOS to look in the directories specified in the path for the file containing the command that has been issued. However, for it to be effective, the path statement must conform to precise rules of structure; as must any entry in the AUTOEXEC.BAT or CONFIG.SYS files.

When DOS receives non-DOS external commands, usually application program files with the EXE or COM extension, it runs them in the resident section of the command processor where, of course, they demand memory. By loading into high memory the operating system and other programs that stay resident when their activity is terminated, more conventional memory is made available for application programs.

Section 4

Component Parts Primer

Introduction

The intention of this section is to familiarize the reader with the various components that will be used to build a computer.

Cases

A wide variety of cases are available including:

- Desktop
- Desktop-slim
- Mini tower
- Mid tower
- Full tower

However, unless the reader has already acquired some technical experience with computers, we recommend against the desktop-slim case because its smaller size tends to make some components difficult to install, and the same argument can be applied to some mini tower cases. The full tower has more than enough space for components, but unless you plan on building a network server there is little point in selecting it. The assembly instructions in this book are based on the most popular, the desktop case, but if you decide on another type you should not have difficulty interpreting the instructions.

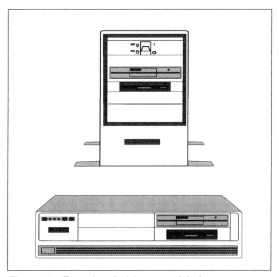

Figure 4-1   Examples of mini tower and desktop cases

Tower cases are usually chosen to be used as file servers on a network. Their desirability in this regard is twofold: first, being more spacious than regular cases, installation of the numerous and often larger components used in a network server is made easier. Second, they can be equipped with two extractor fans, the regular one housed in the power supply, and the other usually located low down at the front. Much heat is generated within a computer and one or more fans are essential, particularly in the case of a heavily loaded file server.

Most desktop cases consist of two main parts; a removable top, and integral front, base, and back plates.

The top can usually be removed by undoing five screws at the back, then sliding the top forward (see Figure 4-2 that follows). Locating guides, in the front inside of the case, may prevent the top section from sliding easily; if this is so, place a pad (for protection) against one of the back, top corners, then strike it sharply with a closed fist. (This is best achieved by leaning over the front of the case, holding the pad with one hand, and striking the corner with the small finger part of the clenched fist of your other hand.) This action will free the top from the guides and allow the top to slide all the way off.

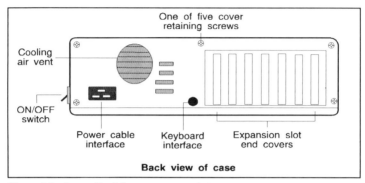

One of five cover
retaining screws

Cooling
air vent

ON/OFF
switch

Power cable
interface

Keyboard
interface

Expansion slot
end covers

Back view of case

Figure 4-2   Case with sliding cover secured at rear

With the many designs available, it may well be that the case you buy dismantles in a different way. Usually, it is not difficult to determine the procedure, but if you experience difficulty, contact the technical help department of the supplier.

Often, cases include power supplies and, in fact, you are advised to buy a case with the power supply included in order to be sure that the designs are complimentary.

Power Supplies

A variety of power supplies are available, in shapes to suit the various cases that are available, and with wattage ratings of 200, 230, and 250. Base your selection of wattage on the intended use of your computer. If you plan on installing the minimum of hardware, choose a 200-watt power supply, but if you plan to load your computer with hardware, go for one of the larger sizes. With the sizes quoted above, you cannot over-power. It is essential to ensure that the model ordered from the supplier will physically fit the case ordered.

With most desktop cases, the power supply fits into the back right-hand corner of the case, with the ON/OFF switch to the right, and the slots in the base-plate of the power supply sliding over the lips protruding from the bottom of the case. The power supply is then secured to the back plate of the case using the screws provided. If the fitting is different and you experience difficulty, do not hesitate to get help from the supplier's technical department.

The power supply has two types of cable connector. The first type supplies power to the motherboard using two sets of six wires each, usually marked P8 and P9. These wires plug into sockets on the motherboard, usually similarly marked, but in the event the identification numbers are not clear, if one set of wires has an orange-colored one, interface that connector first so that the orange wire is closest to the rear of the computer case as shown in Figure 4-3 that follows. If there is no orange-colored wire, refer to the user instructions provided with the power supply to identify the correct cable order. The other sets of wires which provide power to the disk drives have four wires, and there are usually four sets of them; two with regular connectors for 5.25-inch drives and two with mini-connectors for 3.5-inch drives.

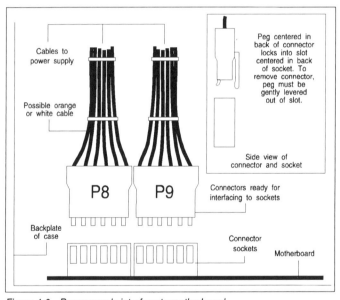

Figure 4-3   Power supply interface to motherboard

A male socket is located at the rear of the power supply to accept the power cable (which is supplied) for bringing power from the wall outlet or surge suppressor.

CAUTION

If the option is provided, ensure that the voltage selector is set to the correct voltage before connecting to an electrical outlet.

Power cables should be connected to a surge protector or an uninterruptable power supply and not directly into wall outlets.

Motherboards

Although motherboards have similar parts, they are often not the same size, which is why the base plate in a computer case offers a variety of locating and securing positions. Most motherboards are located on the base plate of the case by plastic supports described in the following figures.

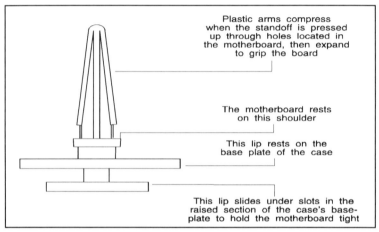

Figure 4-4   Motherboard plastic standoff

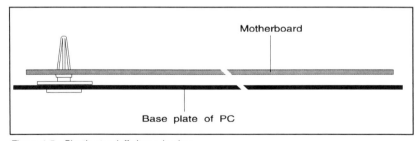

Figure 4-5   Plastic standoff shown in place

To determine where to insert the supports, place the bare motherboard on top of the case base plate so that the keyboard interface socket lines up with the round hole in the back plate of the case, designed to allow the keyboard cable to enter the case. Then observe which holes in the board locate above base plate slots, and which locate over threaded holes for support posts—preferably two, one at the front and one at the back. See Figure 4-6 that follows.

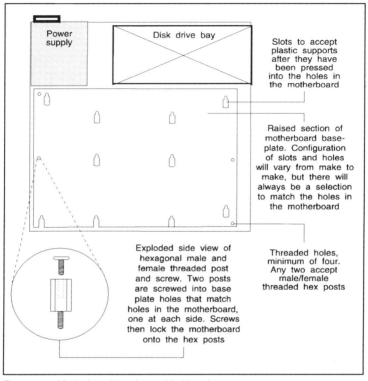

Figure 4-6   Motherboard locating and locking slots

Memory

Memory was discussed and illustrated in Section 3, leaving little more to be said at this point.

SIMM modules and sockets are referred to as "banks" which are numbered 0, 1, 2, etc. (Note that the starting number is zero.) When all the banks are full, the computer is said to be fully populated with memory.

Dipswitches and Jumpers

A motherboard may have either switches (known as dipswitches) or jumpers (which act as switches), or both. Dipswitches are in banks of up to eight or more, as can be jumpers although they are usually found in smaller groupings. Dipswitches are miniature switches, a bank of eight being about one inch long. Jumpers, shown in the following figure, have caps which are about a quarter of an inch in height.

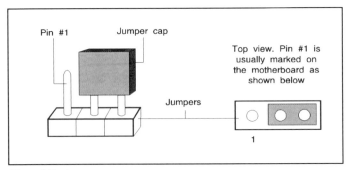

Figure 4-7   Jumpers

Dipswitches and jumpers are used for setting variables such as:

- Color or monochrome video
- Type of RAM
- Number of memory banks used
- Amount of memory
- Processor speed
- Wait states

If there is no cap on a jumper, or if the cap is only on one pin, then the switch is not closed. If a jumper has three pins the center pin is common, and which of the remaining two pins is capped (shorted) will determine, for example, if color video or monochrome is selected.

Uncapped jumpers are also used to make wire connections to the motherboard from the control panel. These wire connections between the motherboard and the control panel are for the purpose of activating the following:

- Speaker
- Power LED (light emitting diode)
- Key lock
- Reset switch
- Speed switch (turbo)
- Turbo LED

The user manual that comes with a motherboard provides details of all dipswitch and jumper selections, as well as wire connections, with jumpers referred to as JP followed by a number, and wire connectors as J followed by a number.

An uncapped jumper is provided for an external battery connection in the event the built-in battery fails. A built-in battery can be replaced, but it involves soldering the connections, which can be a difficult task. The external battery is only external to the motherboard and, when used, is usually attached to the side of the power supply by a Velcro pad.

System BIOS

BIOS chips run an internal diagnostics procedure and, at first power-up after assembly, the BIOS invariably find that the actual (new) configuration does not compare with the default configuration that was read into the CMOS chip when it was first set up. If the BIOS is able to access the video screen (monitor), a message is displayed requesting the user to enter the setup program in order to record the new configuration. However, if the video screen cannot be accessed— possibly because a faulty memory chip is preventing continuance of the diagnostic procedure—then the speaker (if connected properly) will emit a beep or series of beeps, which indicate various malfunctions and allows the user to diagnose the problem and make the necessary corrections.

The following is an example of beep code messages. These do vary from manufacturer to manufacturer, and you should check the user manual or with the supplier.

1 beep—DRAM refresh failure
2 beeps—Parity circuitry failure
3 beeps—First 64KB base memory failure

> 4 beeps—System timer failure
> 5 beeps—Processor failure
> 6 beeps—Keyboard controller failure
> 7 beeps—Virtual mode exception error
> 8 beeps—Display memory read/write test failure
> 9 beeps—ROM BIOS checksum error

On hearing beeps, most readers will be limited to checking to ensure the keyboard and monitor are properly connected or, if you have access to a spare memory module, replacing the installed modules one at a time with the spare one in order to determine if there is a faulty module. Beyond the foregoing, you will need to seek assistance from a local technical source, or from the component parts source. However, you will be relieved to know that these beep code messages are very rare indeed.

If your computer has been properly assembled and boots as far as the screen instruction to enter the setup program, simply follow the instruction, which might read "Press F1 for setup program," or "Press Ctrl, Alt, Escape to enter setup program," or some such similar instruction.

Setup programs will vary with makes and versions of the BIOS chips, but they all accomplish the same minimum, which is:

- Setting time and date on the internal clock/calendar
- Indicating the amount of installed base memory
- Indicating the amount of installed extended memory
- Selecting the specifications of installed floppy drives
- Selecting the specifications of installed hard drives
- Selecting the type of video display card

NOTE

Some makes of BIOS will automatically identify the memory that is installed and also the type of video card.

A typical setup program as it appears on the monitor screen is shown in Figure 4-8 where a fictitious company name has been used. Selection is made by using the arrow keys to move the highlight bar to the desired item and then pressing the Enter key.

```
                    ROM  SETUP  VERSION  4.1
                COPYRIGHT CYBER CHIPS LTD 1995
                      ALL  RIGHTS  RESERVED

          1.    CURRENT  DATE:  [01-30-1995]
          2.    CURRENT  TIME:  [15:35:00]
          3.    COPROCESSOR:    [   1   ]
          4.    BASE  MEMORY:        [ 640   KB]
          5.    EXTENDED  MEMORY:    [7168  KB]
          6.    DISKETTE  DRIVE  A:  [1.44  MB]
                DISKETTE  DRIVE  B:  [  NO   ]
          7.    FIXED  DISK  TYPE  C:[420/IDE ]
                FIXED  DISK  TYPE  D:[  NO   ]
          8.    PRIMARY  DISPLAY  CARD:[  VGA   ]
          9.    EXIT


                CHOOSE ITEM NUMBER: [1]

   - - - - - - - - - - - - - - - - - - - - - - -

    :CHOOSE ITEM        :MODIFY        :ACCEPT
```

Figure 4-8   View of a setup screen

With the advent of simplified but advanced computer graphics, some setup programs project progressively expanding frames after the user makes a selection, with the final frame offering selection choices. When the choice is confirmed, the frames then contract within themselves, revealing the original screen. This information is provided so that a novice will not be alarmed when such activity takes place on the monitor screen.

The extent of the setup program will depend on the make of the BIOS. In addition to the basic setup, the more comprehensive programs will include capabilities such as hard disk initialization, a built-in utility providing such items as a calculator, setting a password, selection of shadow RAM, and number of wait states. However, until a novice user has gained more experience it is wiser to leave these additional programs in their default state.

Floppy Disk Drives

The following figure shows a representation of a 5.25-inch drive with a rail ready to be attached by screws. The rails (one on each side) should be located vertically on the side of the drive so that the drive is flush with the top of the drive bay when the rails engage in the guides. They should also be located horizontally on the side of the drive so that the front of the drive aligns with the front of the case when the computer is fully assembled.

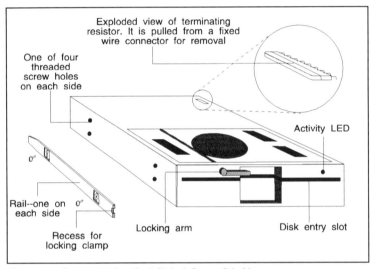

Figure 4-9   Representation of a 5.25-inch floppy disk drive

If a second drive is to be fitted, a drive cover plate may need to be removed from the front of the case's top cover to allow the second drive to slide in immediately below the first.

Some cases are supplied with 3.5-inch bays which accept 3.5-inch drives, but if a 3.5-inch drive is to be installed in a 5.25-inch bay it will need to be mounted in an adapter kit to which the rails can be attached. The adapter kit should be supplied with all 3.5-inch drives (floppy or hard), but it is best to check at the time of placing the order. Detailed assembly instructions are supplied with the kit, and the following figure has been included only to give the reader a preliminary understanding in order to help the flow of these paragraphs.

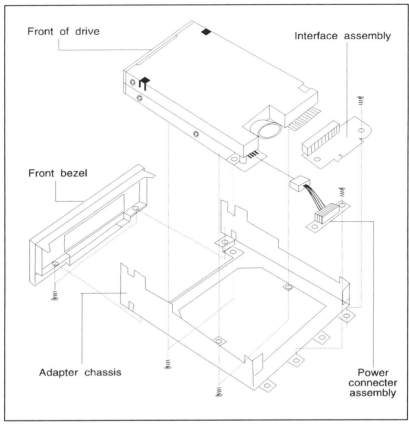

Front of drive

Interface assembly

Front bezel

Adapter chassis

Power connecter assembly

Figure 4-10   3.5-inch disk drive with 5.25-inch adapter kit

Floppy disks, either 3.5-inch or 5.25-inch, should be slid into a drive with the label side up, therefore the drive itself should be installed in the bay the right way up, even though it can function in most any position. The right way for a 5.25-inch drive is with the locking arm uppermost, and for a 3.5-inch drive with the release button at the bottom. When a 3.5-inch disk is inserted in the drive it self-locks and the button must be pressed to eject it. A 5.25-inch disk must be locked in, then when the arm is lifted the disk self-ejects.

Usually, floppy drives (and hard drives) are secured with small right angled plates that are screwed into the front of the case (immediately to the sides of the drive or drive adapter), with the right-angled part clamping into the slotted end of each rail. If the rails have been attached properly to the drives, the back end of the rails will come up hard against stops at the back ends of the rail guides in the bay.

Hard Disk Drives

As described in Section 3, hard disk drives come in a variety of physical sizes as well as storage capacities. Widths are the same as those of floppy disk drives, 5.25 inches and 3.5 inches and heights are 3 inches for a full height and 1.5 inches for a half height. Some computer cases make provision for both widths, while some have bays only suitable for the 5.25-inch. In the former case, a 3.5-inch drive can be adapted to fit into the 5.25-inch bay in the same way as a floppy drive.

In a desktop case, install the hard drive near the bottom in order to give ease of access to the connectors. The rails should be positioned to allow the drive to slide deep into the case so that when the top (and front) cover of the computer case is in place the drive cannot be seen. LED activity is then controlled by a wire connector from the back of the LED to a type of jumper on the hard disk controller (see Figure 4-14 in this section).

Ribbon cables from the disk drive controller and power cables from the power supply connect at the back of the drive. Figure 4-11 is a representation of a 3.5-inch IDE hard drive without rails fitted. It

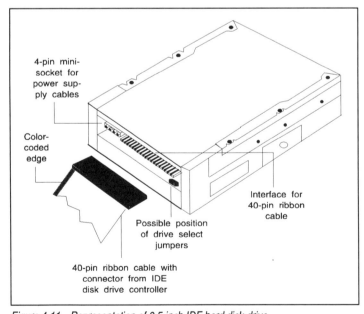

Figure 4-11   Representation of 3.5-inch IDE hard disk drive

shows a 40-pin ribbon cable and connector ready for interfacing and the socket for the power connection. Although hard drives will function in most positions, if a desktop PC is to be stood on one side in a cradle when in operation in order to save space, it is good practice to format the drive in that position.

Hard disks, like floppy disks, must be formatted. However, before formatting, some older hard disks must also be initialized, or low-level formatted, but not those with the IDE interface. Attempting to initialize an IDE hard drive will destroy it.

Beyond the Basics The discussions that follow in this subsection rightly belong in Section 3, and not in this section which deals with the components you will need for assembly. However, while disk structure and defragmentation are not components, they do seem to fit better here and so are included.

Disk Structure

Essentially, DOS treats both floppy and hard disks in the same manner, and the following are definitions of DOS disk structure terminology with some disk hardware terminology included for your convenience. Figure 4-12 following the definitions illustrates disk structure.

- *Platter (or disk)* A magnetically coated metal disk, thin and flexible in a floppy disk, rigid and usually stacked one above the other in a hard disk.
- *Read/write head* The device that moves across the surface of a disk to write information to the disk or to read information from the disk. The head does not touch the disk. Most disks are double sided; thus there are two disk drive read/write heads for each disk.
- *Tracks* Concentric circles on a disk, not spiral as on a phonograph disk, that are numbered from the outside starting at 0. Most floppy disks have either 40 or 80 tracks per side, while hard disks have many more, some as many as 1,000.
- *Cylinders* Tracks of the same DOS number on each platter form a cylinder.
- *DOS Sectors* A sector is that part of a track lying within what could be termed "a pie slice" of the disk. If a disk has nine sectors per track and 40 tracks, then there would be 360 sectors.

- *Storage capacity* Basically dependent on the number of platters, sides, tracks, and sectors. The 5.25-inch DD floppy disk stores 512K on each sector, thus the total storage capacity is 2 (sides) x 40 (tracks per side) x 9 (sectors per track) x 512 (bytes) = 368,640 bytes—usually referred to as a 360K disk.
- *Clusters* A cluster is a set of contiguous sectors. A 360K floppy has two sectors per cluster, while a hard disk may have four or more. DOS allocates disk space by using clusters in an attempt to minimize disk fragmentation.

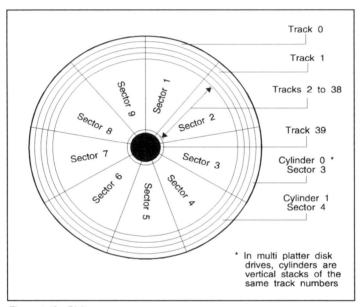

Figure 4-12   Disk structure

- *Disk fragmentation* Generally caused by frequent editing and deletion of files. If a file is enlarged by editing, and if the contiguous cluster next to it has been used, DOS must place the added data in another cluster, either in an unused area of the disk or in the space created by a deleted file. Fragmentation slows down retrieval time because DOS must read from several parts of the disk, one at a time. Figure 4-13 illustrates fragmentation and defragmentation.

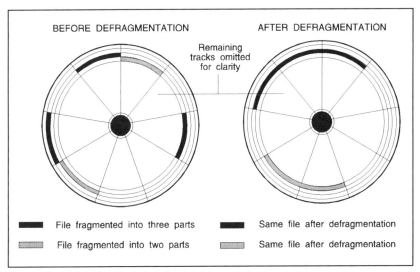

BEFORE DEFRAGMENTATION

AFTER DEFRAGMENTATION

Remaining
tracks omitted
for clarity

File fragmented into three parts

Same file after defragmentation

File fragmented into two parts

Same file after defragmentation

Figure 4-13   Simplified illustration of disk defragmentation

- *Directory entry*   The DOS number of the first cluster in a file and an indicator for the file allocation table (FAT).
- *FAT*   This table contains an entry for each cluster, whether used, available, or corrupted, and is used by DOS for allocating file space and for locating existing files for retrieval.

Floppy and Hard Disk Drive Controllers

Disk drives need controllers. Controllers are in the form of adapter cards or, in the case of floppy drives, they may be an integral part of the motherboard. In the latter case, if a hard drive is installed, a hard drive controller will also be required. If the motherboard does not have floppy drive control capabilities, then a floppy/hard drive controller must be installed in the form of an adapter card.

The IDE interface mini-card shown at Figure 4-14 not only controls two floppy and two hard drives, but also provides multi-I/O functions.

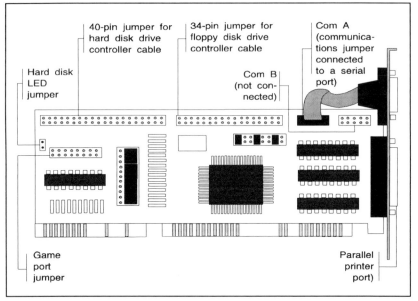

Figure 4-14   16-bit IDE controller and multi-I/O card

Some non-IDE controller cards have their own BIOS chip with a program incorporated for initializing hard disks. Informative booklets are usually provided with such cards, which give step-by-step low-level formatting instructions. Proprietary and other software is also available for low-level formatting, such as:

- Speedstor
- Programs built into the BIOS setup utility
- The DOS DEBUG program

Most non-IDE hard disks are initialized using different sets of fundamental parameters (the drive interface) that relate to specific types of controllers such as MFM, RLL, or ESDI which were described in Section 3. Controllers and hard drives are best purchased together in order to avoid conflict with the drive interface. (A floppy disk drive can be managed by any floppy/hard controller regardless of the hard drive interface.)

Disk Drive Ribbon Cables

Ribbon cables interface the drives to the controller card. Although there are, as usual, several different designs we are only interested in the four types which are in common use in IBM-compatible PCs. They are:

- 34-pin controller ribbon cable for up to two floppy disk drives
- 34-pin controller ribbon cable for up to two non-IDE hard disk drives
- 20-pin data ribbon cable for each non-IDE hard disk drive
- 40-pin controller cable for up to two IDE hard disk drives

Figure 4-15 is an illustration of a 34-pin controller cable for two floppy drives. Not shown are the 34 wires that are soldered to the 34 pins in each of the connectors and which are embedded in the plastic ribbon cable. However, the illustration docs show a section of the cable housing wires 10 through 16 that has been slit open and twisted before entering the first floppy drive connector.

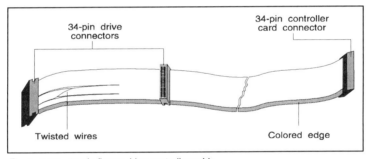

Figure 4-15   34-pin floppy drive controller cable

The twisting technique in a ribbon cable is required when two drives are used and it becomes necessary for the disk controller to be able to address both drives individually, rather than as a pair. However, a single drive will function using either of the connectors on this cable—twisted or not twisted. Cables with only one floppy drive connector are available, and they do not have the twisted section.

A 34-pin controller cable for two non-IDE hard drives differs from the illustration only in that the twist takes place at wires 19 through 25. Thus the different cables can be easily recognized by the position of the twist relative to the colored edge strip, which is always on the same side. A single hard drive may also use this type of cable. The IDE 40-pin cable does not have a twist.

20-pin data cables with a single connector at each end are for non-IDE hard drives only, and each hard drive requires one of these cables.

20-pin and 34-pin non-IDE hard drive connectors interface into the back of the hard drive, as does the IDE 40-pin (shown at Figure 4-11). 34-pin floppy drive connectors interface at the back of floppy drives.

The connectors at the other end of 20-, 34-, and 40-pin cables interface with pin jumpers on controller cards. Figure 4-14 illustrates pin jumpers on an IDE card.

As with jumpers on all boards and cards, pin #1 is so marked on controller cards, and when interfacing a ribbon cable the position of the colored edge should correspond with pin #1.

In the case of the drive interface, there is often a slot toward one side of the strip jumper and a bridge toward one side of the connector, making it impossible to interface the wrong way. With the controller connectors, if the jumper pins on the card are vertical, pin #1 is invariably at the top of the card. Where the jumpers are horizontal, as shown in Figure 4-14, pin #1 is invariably toward the front of the computer when the card is installed.

Speaker

A speaker is not only required to give beep codes if the boot fails, but also for signaling information in application programs, particularly in respect to illegal keyboard commands. Although the speaker has poor fidelity, it can synthesize voice and music.

The speaker will be found in the accessories package that comes with the case, together with a plastic holder for affixing it to the computer case, as shown in Figure 4-16.

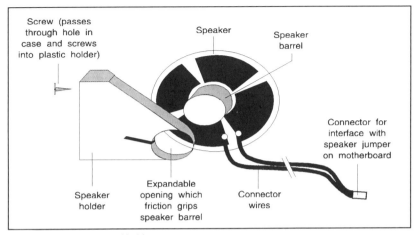

Figure 4-16   Speaker and holder

The barrel of the speaker presses into an expandable opening in the holder which grips it tightly, then the holder is screwed to the wall of the computer case and the connecting wires are interfaced to the appropriate jumper on the motherboard.

In addition to the screw hole in the base of the holder, there is a small locating peg that fits into a prepared hole on one of the front left walls of the computer case. When in place, the holder will project off the wall sideways.

The most common positions for the speaker are either off the front wall of the case, just to the left of the adapter card guides on the cage that protects the back of the control panel LEDs and buttons, or inside the cage, parallel with the front of the case and projecting off the left wall of the cage. When assembling a computer for the first time, it may be necessary to use some ingenuity in locating positions for the assembly of some accessories. Try offering up the speaker holder to various positions until you find one with a screw hole and a peg hole that match those of the holder.

Video Cards

The video card is the major player in the series of events that convert the touch of a keyboard or mouse button into activity on the monitor screen. The most simple and lowest cost video card is a non-graphics monochrome that produces characters only on a green, amber, or white screen. Next in line, illustrated in the following figure is the monochrome graphics card (often called a Hercules graphics card after the name of a manufacturer) which will produce both characters and graphics on a monochrome monitor. These cards have ports for a 9-pin monitor cable and a 25-pin parallel printer cable. (More than one parallel printer port may be installed in a PC.)

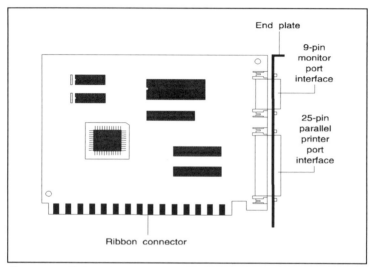

Figure 4-17   Typical 8-bit monographics card

Going to color brings forth some confusion in the terminology applied to the various cards that are available. One of the early color cards (and monitor) is called CGA (Color Graphics Adapter), but this card (as with the simplest monochrome card) offers inferior resolution. Progressing to the EGA (Enhanced Graphics Adapter), resolution is improved to 640 x 350 pixels. Next in line is the VGA (Video Graphics Array) card, with 8-bit versions offering 640 x 480 resolution, and 16-bit Super VGA cards going as high as 1024 x 768—these are the cards that are now usually supplied with off-the-shelf PCs. Video cards for the larger screens used for DTP or CAD applications can provide resolutions up to 1200 x 1600 and beyond.

The number of colors that could be controlled with the earlier color graphics cards was very limited, but the modern VGA cards can provide from 16 to 256 colors, while the specialist cards for DTP and CAD go up to literally millions of colors.

Many video cards have memory chips installed, and in order to enhance resolution, increase the number of colors displayed, and speed up screen refresh time, provision is often made for more memory chips to be added.

Most of the higher-end color video cards have a single 15-pin port, some older ones may also have a 9-pin port to enable the card to be used in the monochrome mode. None of these cards have printer ports, making it necessary for a specific printer card or a multi-I/O card to be installed. Figure 4-18 that follows illustrates a typical high-end VGA card.

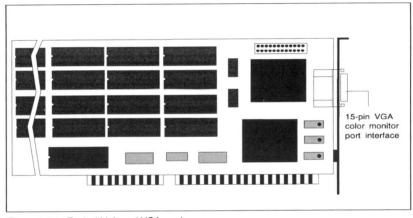

15-pin VGA color monitor port interface

Figure 4-18   Typical high-end VGA card

Multi-I/O Cards

The reader will recall from earlier discussion on BIOS chips that "IO" means "input/output." A multi-I/O card is an adapter card that provides extra ports for both the input and output of data. The following figure shows an I/O card with a game port and a parallel printer port. The function of the game port is to provide an interface for the type of connector found on joy sticks, which are used for controlling video games.

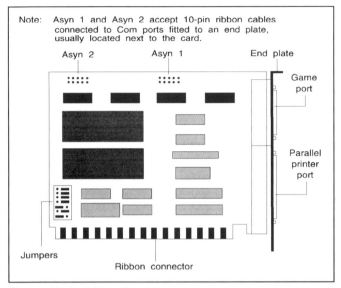

Figure 4-19 *Multi-I/O card*

Switches, which may be jumpers, allow the printer port to be designated LPT1 or LPT2 (DOS reserved names, with LPT being a contraction of Local Printer), useful if two printers are to be connected when there is already a primary printer card.

Other ports for communication are provided on a separate end plate, with each port having a narrow ribbon cable exiting from the back of the port. The other end terminates with 10-pin connectors that interface with the 10-pin jumpers shown in Figure 4-19 as Asyn 1 and Asyn 2. These names refer to Asynchronous Communication Ports which are better known as COM1 or COM2 (DOS reserved names that are contractions of communication). Most multi-I/O card kits include these two ports and their cables, together with full instructions for configuring the ports if for any reason the default settings are not acceptable.

Accelerator Cards

The accelerator card, also known as speed card or Windows accelerator, is a video card designed for high-speed, high-resolution graphics, particularly when animation and full-motion video aspects are involved. A monitor depends upon a video card to send it signals to define pixels. A pixel is one illuminated phosphor dot on the screen. The video card retains in its memory every pixel on the screen and instructs the monitor which ones are to be illuminated. Using an electron beam, the monitor scans each line of pixels on the back of the screen horizontally, starting at the top left and then working down the screen from left to right. When it receives an instruction from the video card to illuminate a pixel, it projects an electron which causes the phosphor of the pixel to glow momentarily. In a color monitor, each pixel contains a dot of each primary color, therefore the video card must be capable of issuing many more instructions than it does for a single color display. It must also be able to instruct the monitor to illuminate more than one dot of color in a pixel at a time in order to make other colors, or partially illuminate a dot(s) of color in a pixel in order to produce shades of a color, and there are millions of shades of color. When animation or full-motion is called for, the electron beam in the monitor must move very much faster to avoid flicker, and it is the video card that controls speed.

An accelerator card, with its advanced video architecture and extremely fast video memory (VRAM), supplies the necessary punch to the monitor to make it capable of displaying full-color, full-motion animation. In appearance, an accelerator card resembles a high-end VGA card but with many more chips. Many accelerator cards are designed for use in the VL-bus which provides for faster processing speed.

Sound Cards

A sound card allows you to record sound in a file in your PC and then to reproduce that sound through the PC's speaker(s), either internal or external. The card is similar in size to a full-size video card but is loaded with electronic gadgetry. It has ports for joystick, microphone, and speakers. With the correct software, you can embed sound (voice or music) into a document. Here's how it works.

When sound passes through your PC's microphone, it passes through a coding/decoding chip on the sound card. Analog values such as frequency and amplitude are established by an algorithm and then converted to binary language. The sound is now in digital form which can be stored in a file on disk. When you wish to play back the sound, the procedure is reversed, but with the signals being sent to speakers.

Keyboards

You may come across two basic types of keyboards, the 84-key and the 101-key, with the principal difference being that in the 84-key board there are no independent scrolling keys.

Some older model keyboards were designed to function with an advanced version of the old 8088 CPU known as the XT, and also with 80286, 386, and 486 CPUs. Such keyboards are switchable, either by automatic sensing or manual control as shown in Figure 4-20.

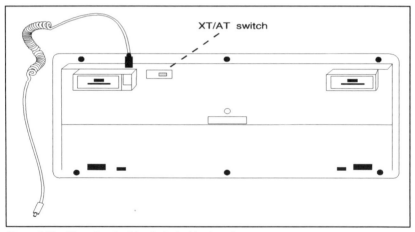

Figure 4-20   View of underside of a typical keyboard

One of the most modern keyboards is marketed by Microsoft. Known as the Natural Keyboard, it is of ergonomic design with a curved console designed to eliminate what is known as carpel tunnel syndrome: pains that occur in the wrists as a result of holding one's hands in an unnatural position for long periods of time.

Section 5

What to Buy

Your Shopping List

Because of the numerous PC configuration choices available, in the tables that follow, shopping lists are given for four basic designs with separate lists for monitors, hard drives, and adapter cards. These basic IBM-compatible PCs are:

- 386DX-40MHz ISA bus
- 486SX-33MHz ISA bus
- 486DX-40MHz ISA bus
- 486DX2-80MHz ISA bus with three VESA local bus slots
- Pentium 66MHz ISA bus with three VESA local bus slots

Table 5-1   386DX-40MHz ISA bus system prices

Description	Price -US$
Desktop case with 200-watt power supply and LED control panel	$ 45
386DX-40MHz motherboard with 128K cache (Phoenix, AMI, or DTK BIOS recommended)	99
4MB 70ns or faster SIMM memory	135
Keyboard (101-key recommended)	26
1.44MB floppy disk drive	32
Set of ribbon cables	10
Microsoft-compatible mouse	29
DOS v6.2	65
	TOTAL $441

Table 5-2   486SX-33MHz ISA bus system prices

Description	Price -US$
Desktop case with 200-watt power supply and LED control panel	$ 45
486SX-33MHz motherboard (Phoenix, AMI, or DTK BIOS recommended)	79
4MB 70ns or faster SIMM memory	135
Keyboard (101-key recommended)	26
1.44MB floppy disk drive	32
Set of ribbon cables	10
Microsoft-compatible mouse	29
DOS v6.2	65
	TOTAL $421

Table 5-3   486DX-40MHz ISA bus system prices

Description	Price -US$
Desktop case with 200-watt power supply and LED control panel	$ 45
486DX-40MHz motherboard (Phoenix, AMI, or DTK BIOS recommended)	139
4MB 70ns or faster SIMM memory	135
Keyboard (101-key recommended)	26
1.44MB floppy disk drive	32
Set of ribbon cables	10
Microsoft-compatible mouse	29
DOS v6.2	65
	TOTAL $491

Table 5-4   486DX2-80MHz ISA bus with 3 VESA slots system prices

Description	Price -US$
Desktop case with 230-watt power supply and LED control panel	$ 57
486DX2-80MHz motherboard with 256K cache, 4 ISA slots, and 3 VESA local bus slots (Phoenix, AMI, or DTK BIOS recommended)	415
8MB 70ns or faster SIMM memory	270
Keyboard (101-key recommended)	26
1.44MB floppy disk drive	32
Set of ribbon cables	10
Microsoft-compatible mouse	29
DOS v6.2	65
	TOTAL $904

Table 5-5   Pentium 66MHz ISA bus with 3 VESA slots system prices

Description	Price -US$
Desktop case with 230-watt power supply and LED control panel	$ 57
OPTI Pentium 66MHz motherboard with 256K cache, 4 ISA slots, and 3 VESA local bus slots	998
16MB 60ns SIMM memory	580
Keyboard (101-key recommended)	26
1.44MB floppy disk drive	32
Internal double-speed CD ROM drive	139
Set of ribbon cables	10
Microsoft-compatible mouse	29
DOS v6.2	65
	TOTAL $1,936

Table 5-6 Monitor and hard disk drive prices

MONITORS	Price -US$
14-inch VGA (paper white), 1024x768 pixel resolution, 39 mm dot pitch	$108
14-inch Super VGA color, 1024x768 pixel resolution, 28 mm dot pitch	$219
17-inch Super VGA color (flat tube), 1280x1024 pixel resolution, 28 mm dot pitch	$639
HARD DRIVES	
Conner 210MG IDE, 14ms	$154
Western Digital 340MG IDE, 12ms	$198
Western Digital 425MG IDE, 12ms	$219
Western Digital 540MG (dual platter) IDE, 11ms	$265

Notes:

1. Your computer must have a monitor, a video card, a floppy drive and controller.

2. Order hard drive rails if not supplied with case.

3. There are larger and more sophisticated monitors and hard drives available.

Table 5-7 Adapter card prices

ADAPTER CARDS	Price -US$
Multi-I/O	
8-bit with 2 serial, 1 parallel, and 1 game port	$12
Drive Controller	
16-bit ISA IDE with 2 floppy and 2 hard drives	$14
32-bit VESA Super-IDE with 2 floppy, 2 hard drives, and multi-I/O	$18
Video and Video/Accelerator	
16-bit ISA bus Video (1024x768) with 512K RAM	$38
16-bit Trident ISA bus Video (1024x768) with 1MB RAM (16.8 million colors)	$62
32-bit Cirrus VESA local bus Video/Accelerator (16.8 million colors) with 2MB D-RAM	$67
32-bit Diamond Stealth VESA local bus Video/ Accelarator (16.8 million colors) with 2MB D-RAM	$199
32-bit Diamond Stealth VESA local bus Video/ Accelarator (16.8 million colors) with 4MB V-RAM	$459
Sound	
16-bit Midas stereo sound (low-end card)	$99
32-bit Turtle Beach stereo (high-end card)	$449
Modems	
2400 Baud internal modem	$15
28.8K Internal FAX and modem	$115

NOTES: 1. Your computer must have a monitor, a video card, a floppy drive and controller.

2. There are more sophisticated and more powerful adapter cards available.

Prices are typical "wholesale to the public" and were current at the time of printing. However, they may vary from supplier to supplier and should be used as a guide only. Shipping costs may be extra. Orders from out-of-town suppliers are usually shipped by road parcel carrier, COD against cash or cashier's check.

Retail prices for assembled name-brand systems, often sold through department and superstores, may not be a great deal higher than what a similar system will cost you to build. However, such deals are usually for systems of specific configurations and may not be exactly what you want. Systems can also be purchased by mail, ready assembled at seemingly low prices, but you get what you pay for and the low cost ones do not always prove to be the lowest cost in the long run. Assembling your own computer not only allows you to configure it exactly how you want it, but also provides valuable experience that will stand you in good stead when the time comes to repair or upgrade.

Sources

Of the many computer parts distributors in the United States, a number are genuine wholesalers who will not supply unless you are able to quote them an authentic sales tax number. Good prices are available from national retail stores such as CompUSA. You should also consult your Yellow Pages for wholesale suppliers with local stores who will deal with the public, one such is Micromax Distribution. *Computer Shopper* magazine, available from book and magazine stores, is a good source for obtaining prices and names of suppliers, but you may find it necessary to weed out the good from the bad. Other sources are computer shows which are staged fairly regularly in most cities.

Notes:

1. Be aware that different makes and models of computer components are likely to vary in design and appearance. As a result, the reader may find it necessary to adapt the assembly instructions to suit a particular make or model. However, the assembly instructions have been written with this ambiguity in mind, and no serious difficulties should arise.

2. If a non-IDE hard disk drive is ordered, request the following specification information, which may be needed for initializing. (Abbreviated descriptions are given in parentheses.):

   - Number of cylinders (CYL)
   - Number of heads (HEADS)
   - Write precompensation cylinder (CYLINDERS)
   - Landing Zone (LZ)
   - Drive's physical sectors/track (SECTORS)

3. You must buy MS-DOS from the store where you buy your case and motherboard because DOS is not otherwise available unless you buy a new system. Upgrades are available, but unless you already have DOS installed in another system they will do you no good because a boot disk is not supplied. If you have DOS installed elsewhere, make a boot disk for use following assembly of your new PC.

4. A new alternative to the VESA local bus for Pentium systems is known as PCI, and if the Pentium-powered PC becomes commonplace, PCI may push VESA into the background. If you decide to go with a Pentium CPU, discuss PCI with your supplier.

Section 6

Assembly Instructions

Preparation

Tools

The first three of the tools listed are essential for the assembly. The others that are listed are desirable but not essential.

- No. 2 Phillips screwdriver
- Flat blade screwdriver
- Needle nose pliers
- Tweezers
- Magnifying glass
- Flashlight
- Small containers for loose screws, etc.
- Magnet (useful to magnetize screwdrivers in order to prevent screws falling into case where they could short out circuits, but keep all magnets and magnetized objects well away from floppy and hard disks)

Workspace

Minimum of 6' x 3' work table is desirable.

Power

Regular electric supply from wall outlet protected by a surge protector. Surge protectors are available from computer parts suppliers, electrical supply stores, hardware stores, and some office equipment stores.

Components

Unpack cartons and ensure that no component is damaged. In the event of damage or malfunction, either take it back to the supplier or call the supplier and obtain an RMA # (returned merchandise number). Repack the part in the original packing, and clearly mark the RMA # on the outside of the carton.

Lay out component parts in a logical order in a safe area such as on another table.

Case

Remove appropriate screws from the case (see Figure 4-2 in Section 4), then slide off cover and place it out of the way.

Retrieve accessories package from inside the case, then sort and store contents in separate containers. Contents will usually consist of:

- Control panel assembly if not already fitted
- Interface slot end plates
- Small, flat and right-angled drive clamps
- Keys
- Motherboard metal hex support posts
- Motherboard plastic standoffs
- Plastic guides for end of adapter cards. (Guides press into holes in cage on front inside wall of case. Select logical way up so that cards will slide in easily.)
- Rails for disk drives
- Round rubber feet
- Screws
- Speaker and holder
- Two sizes of oval ended plates for closing off unused interface port outlets in back wall of case

Assembly

Case

1. Affix rubber feet to base of case, set in about two inches from the corners.

Power Supply

1. If not supplied pre-installed, remove power supply from its carton, setting the main power cable to one side. With a desktop case, position the power supply in the back, right-hand corner of the open case with the ON/OFF switch to the outside.

2. Engage the slots on the under surface of the power supply with the lips on the raised base plate of the case, then push the power supply until it is flush with the PC's back plate.

3. Identify suitable screws and secure the power supply to the back plate of the case from the outside.

Speaker

1. Assemble the speaker and holder. Identify the correct position for the holder (usually on the cage that accepts plastic guides to hold the ends of full-length adapter cards), and secure with appropriate screw (see Figure 4-16 in Section 4).

Control Panel

1. If not already installed, use suitable screws to secure the control panel sub-assembly to the front plate of the open computer case (usually near the top left corner). Before securing it in position, lead the wires through the cutout in the front plate and then out the side of the cage nearest the drive bays.

Memory

1. Install the SIMM module(s) in the SIMM sockets of the banks you plan using on the motherboard. To do this, orient the first module so that the notches in the module and the socket are at the same end (see Figure 3-5 in Section 3).

2. Hold the module in two hands and offer it to the socket, leaning it back slightly. Observe the metal spring clips at each end of the socket that are designed to lock into small holes at each end of the module. Push the module into the socket as you slowly bring it to the vertical, forcing it past the spring clips which should then lock into the holes.

Tip If you find the foregoing procedure difficult to accomplish, have someone hold the clips open to facilitate getting the module into the vertical position and seating it firmly in the socket. The clips must be securely home in the module holes, otherwise a memory fault may occur when you switch on the computer.

3. Repeat the procedure for any other SIMM memory modules you wish to install.

Motherboard

1. With the motherboard populated with memory, orient the computer case so that the left side is toward the front of the work table.

2. Hold the motherboard so that the expansion slots are to the left, then offer the motherboard to the base plate of the case to identify the best positions for the insertion of the plastic standoffs and the locations of the metal hex posts (see Figure 4-6 in Section 4).

3. Insert the plastic standoffs into the holes you selected in the motherboard, pushing them up from the bottom (see Figures 4-4 and 4-5 in Section 4).

4. Identify screws for at least two metal hex posts, then screw the posts into the selected places on the raised base plate of the case. Tighten with pliers or a wrench.

5. Refer to the user manual that came with the motherboard and set all jumpers and/or dipswitches to conform to your chosen computer configuration. Identify the jumpers and connectors that will interface the speaker and the control panel LEDs and buttons to the motherboard.

6. Position the motherboard just above the raised base plate of the case, about half an inch back from the ultimate position, then lower it so that the plastic standoffs drop into the wide parts of the slots in the base plate. Work the board forward until the threaded holes of the metal hex posts can be seen through the appropriate holes in the motherboard.

7. Using a Phillips screwdriver, secure the board in position using the previously identified screws. Proof positive that the board is correctly located will be by checking that the keyboard interface is lined up accurately with the round hole in the back wall of the case.

Tip You may find the foregoing procedure difficult to accomplish because one or more plastic standoffs may snag and prevent the board from sliding into position. Because you cannot easily see which standoff has snagged, it is best to remove the board and start again. Practice does make perfect.

Power Supply Connectors

1. Correctly align the power supply connectors with their sockets, either with the P8 and P9 identifying numbers or by cable identity as described in Section 4.

2. With the connectors properly aligned, grip the connector that is nearest thc back plate of the computer, and position it immediately above the end of the ribbon connector socket also nearest the back plate. (See Figure 4-3 in Section 4.)

3. Tilt the top of the connector away from the power supply and engage the pegs on the connector with the small slots in the socket. Straighten the connector while pressing down to complete a secure interface. Repeat procedure for second connector.

Control Panel Connections

1. Interface the connectors by first identifying the wire color code as it emerges from the back of the LED, button, or lock. Then, refer to the motherboard user manual and identify the live wires and the ground wires.

2. Identify the #1 pin of the jumper you plan to interface (it is better to start with the jumper furthest away from the side of the computer case which was aligned with the front of the table—see motherboard instructions) and orient the connector according to the manual instructions (usually with the live wire to the #1 pin).

3. Carefully push the connector over the jumper pins until it is fully seated. Repeat the procedure for all the connectors except for the hard disk drive LED.

4. Tidy up the wires, securing them with a tie or string to ensure they are unlikely to become entangled with other components.

Floppy Disk Drive

1. If your computer case is fitted with 3.5-inch bays, install the 3.5-inch floppy drive directly into the top right bay so that it will be flush with the front of the computer cover when the cover is replaced. (The disk release button should be at the bottom.) Secure the drive at the sides with screws.

2. If your computer case is fitted with 5.25-inch drive bays, mount the 3.5-inch floppy drive in the 5.25-inch adapter kit in accordance with the provided instructions. (Also see Figure 4-10 in Section 4.)

3. Identify four screws that will fit the threads in the holes on the sides of the frame and which will also fit flush into the recesses in the side of the rails (see Figures 4-9 and 4-10 in Section 4).

4. Install rails on the drive adapter frame. Then turn the computer to face the front of the table and install the adapter and drive, with the rails mating with the top rail guides in the main drive bay. If the drive is not flush with the top of the bay, adjust the vertical position of the rails until it is.

5. When pushed back as far as it will go in the bay, the drive should be flush with the front of the computer cover where the closure panel was removed. You may need to temporarily fit the cover to check drive positioning. Adjust the position of the rails on the drive vertically and horizontally if necessary to achieve the correct position.

6. Secure the drive using flat or right-angled drive clamps so that the lugs engage in the recesses in the end of the rails.

7. Interface one of the power cable mini-connectors to the 4-pin socket of the floppy drive. Stow the other cables out of the way for the time being.

Video Card

1. Refer to the instruction sheet or booklet supplied with the video card and ensure that dipswitches and jumpers (if any) are set to conform to the system configuration.

2. Select a suitable expansion slot, preferably one at or near the edge of the motherboard furthest from the power supply. (See Figure 3-7 in Section 3.) If it is a 32-bit local bus card, be sure you select a local bus slot.

3. Grip the card firmly between fingers and thumb, avoiding fragile devices and sharp-ended wires. Press the card firmly into the selected slot, making sure that its end plate fits behind the motherboard at the bottom and over the back plate of the case at the top. Ensure that the bronze-colored connector strip on the card seats in the slot and not to one side.

4. Lock the card in position with a screw passing through its end plate and into the back plate of the case.

IDE Disk Controller Card

1. Following the basic procedure for the video card, install this card in a 16-bit slot as near to the main drive bay as possible in order to simplify subsequent cable connections. If it is a composite multi-I/O card, fit the loose end plate next to the controller card and make the ribbon connections.

2. Interface the hard disk drive indicator wire (usually red and white) with the jumper on the end of the controller card. (See Figure 4-14 in Section 4.)

3. Interface the floppy drive ribbon cable (see Figure 4-15 in Section 4) to the floppy drive and the other end to the controller (see Figure 4-14 and associated text in Section 4). The second drive connector on the ribbon cable will only be used if a second floppy drive is subsequently installed.

NOTE

A hard drive, and the second floppy drive if one is desired, will be installed after the system has been booted on a single drive in order to minimize troubleshooting in the event of a failed boot.

Keyboard

1. Check to ensure that if there is a switch or dipswitches on the back of the board that they are correctly set. (See Figure 4-20 in Section 4 and associated text.)

2. Position the keyboard on the table in front of the computer, then lead the cable to the back of the computer and complete the interface. An indentation on the keyboard cable connector should be to the top when the connector is pushed home.

Monitor

1. Position the monitor on the table to the left of the computer. If not already connected to the monitor, interface the video cable and the power cable in accordance with the manufacturer's instructions.

2. Interface the free end of the video cable to the port on the video card where it projects through the back plate of the computer.

3. Interface the free end of the power cable into a surge protector connected to an electrical wall outlet, or directly into an electrical wall outlet.

4. Switch on the monitor and check that the activity light comes on if there is one, then switch it off.

Congratulations, your new computer is now ready for booting, which is covered in the following section. Proceed directly to that section if you are familiar with DOS, otherwise first study "DOS for Beginners" in Section 11 and then return to Section 7 for booting instructions.

Section 7

Booting

Safety Check

1. Ensure all loose tools, wires, screws, etc., are removed from the computer and its immediate surrounds.
2. Recheck all installations, connections, and interfaces that have been made. In fact, run a check list using the assembly instructions.
3. If there is a voltage selection switch on the power supply, ensure it is switched to the correct reading (110v in the United States).

Powering Up

1. Check that the main power switch on the computer is off.
2. Interface the female connector end of the power cable (supplied with the power supply) to the socket at the rear of the computer (at the power supply position). Insert the other end of the power cable into the surge protector or directly into a wall outlet if a surge protector is not available.
3. Switch on the monitor.
4. Insert a DOS boot disk into the floppy disk drive, ensuring that the correct side is up. If it is a 5.25-inch disk, close the locking arm.
5. Power up the computer. (Turn on the computer's main power switch.)

Monitoring the Boot

1. If everything is in order, the boot will progress to a monitor screen instruction to enter the setup program, which may be similar to Figure 4-8 in Section 4. Also see associated text in that section.

2. Follow screen instructions and enter details of the computer's configuration. When complete, the setup program will reboot the computer to record the changes. Your monitor may display diagnostic checks similar to those shown in Figure 7-1. Then the DOS disk will be read until a screen prompt asks for the current time and date. Respond by pressing the Enter key at each prompt to override the requests, then power down, remove and store the DOS disk, and proceed to Section 8 to install a second floppy drive and/or a hard drive.

```
486DX-SUPERCHECK-03  Modular  BIOS  Version  4.0
Copyright  1992-94  Super  Software  Inc.
486DX  Version  4.2P

TESTING  INTERRUPT  CONTROLLER  #1 ..................... PASS
TESTING  INTERRUPT  CONTROLLER  #2 ..................... PASS
TESTING  CMOS  BATTERY ................................. PASS
TESTING  CMOS  CHECKSUM ................................ PASS
SIZING  SYSTEM  MEMORY......................... 640K  FOUND
TESTING  SYSTEM  MEMORY ....................... 640K  PASS
CHECKING  UNEXPECTED  INTERRUPTS  AND  STUCK  NMI ..PASS
TESTING  PROTECTED  MODE .............................. PASS
SIZING  EXTENDED  MEMORY ..................... 03072K  FOUND
TESTING  MEMORY  IN  PROTECTED  MODE ........ 03712K  PASS
TESTING  PROCESSOR  EXCEPTION  INTERRUPTS ........... PASS
BIOS  SHADOW  RAM .................................. ENABLED
VIDEO  SHADOW  RAM ................................. ENABLED

<PRESS  CTRL+ALT+ESC  FOR  SETUP>
```

Figure 7-1   Example of BIOS diagnostic checks

Troubleshooting a Failed Boot

1. It is important to power down before making any changes to the configuration of a computer.

2. If at any time your corrective actions result in a successful boot, proceed to Section 8.

3. If there are no warning beeps, nothing on the monitor screen, and the front power LED is out, check the following:

   a. That the wall outlet is active

   b. That the surge protector is active

   c. That the power supply fan is running (check by ear)

Tip If it seems certain that power is reaching the computer's power supply but the fan is not running, the unit could be faulty and may require replacing.

4. If the power supply fan is running, power down and check the following:

   a. All connections and interfaces inside the computer

   b. The monitor power cable and video cable connections

   c. All dipswitches and jumpers for correct settings

   d. All LED and button connections from the control panel to ensure that they are interfaced with the correct jumpers and oriented properly

   e. All memory chips to ensure that the modules are properly seated and that the correct banks have been populated

NOTE

Keep in mind that if all components are correctly installed, failure to boot as a result of component failure is very rare. A more likely cause is faulty installation. However, if all possible rectification procedures fail, communicate with the supplier in order to obtain assistance from their technical support department.

5. If the system emits a series of beeps, power down and check the following:

   a. That the appropriate dipswitches and/or jumpers are set to match the amount and type of installed RAM

   b. That the correct memory banks have been populated

   c. That the notches in the modules and sockets match

   d. That the modules are correctly installed

   e. That the modules are not damaged. Remove all the modules for damage inspection, then replace them carefully if they seem to be serviceable.

    f. That the keyboard is connected to the computer

    g. That if configurable, the keyboard switch is set correctly

    h. That the video cable is properly connected

    i. That the video card is fully seated in the correct size slot

    j. That all dipswitches and/or jumpers are correctly set

6. If you are still unable to rectify the fault, seek help from your supplier's technical support department.

Section 8

Installing Additional Drives

Installing a CD ROM Drive

Install according to the drive manufacturer's instructions, referring to the steps for installing a second floppy drive where appropriate.

Installing a Second Floppy Disk Drive

Perform the step that follows to remove an appropriate panel from the plastic front cover of the computer in order to expose a second drive.

1. Remove two holding screws from the inside of the cover, or spring the panel out if there are no screws.

It is assumed that the second drive you intend to install, if not a CD ROM, will be a 5.25-inch floppy in a 5.25-inch bay. If the 3.5-inch floppy drive you installed was in a 5.25-inch adapter, it will be installed in the top right bay, and you should install the second drive immediately below it. If the 3.5-inch drive was installed in a 3.5-inch bay, then use the nearest convenient 5.25-inch bay for the second floppy drive. Perform the steps that follow to install the drive.

1. If one is fitted, remove the terminating resistor from the drive that is not to be the last drive. (See Figure 4-9 in Section 4.)

2. Identify four screws that will fit the threads in the holes on the sides of the drive, and which will also fit flush into the recesses in the sides of the rails.

3. Orient the drive so that the disk release lever is at the top. Then fit rails to the sides of the drive (see Figure 4-9 in Section 4) so that when the drive is in the bay the front will fit where the closure panel was removed from the computer's cover. You may

need to temporarily fit the cover to check drive positioning. Adjust the position of the rails on the drive vertically and horizontally if necessary to achieve the correct position.

4. Secure the drive using flat or right-angled drive clamps so that the lugs engage in the recesses in the ends of the rails.

5. Interface one of the power cable connectors to the 4-pin socket of the floppy drive, and interface the second connector on the floppy drive ribbon cable to the drive.

6. Insert the DOS boot disk into drive A and boot the computer. It will again be necessary to enter the setup program in order to record details of the second drive.

7. If after installation DOS will not recognize the drive, try switching the ribbon cable connectors from one floppy drive to the other, but if that is unsuccessful, check with the supplier's technical support department to determine if the particular drive to be used will need reconfiguring in order to function as drive B.

Installing an IDE Hard Disk Drive

1. Install the drive into a 5.25-inch adapter kit, following the procedure described for a 3.5-inch floppy drive.

2. Fit rails to the adapter frame, but position them so that the front of the drive is flush with the front of the drive bay and not the front panel of the computer. The intention here is that the drive will not be visible when the computer is fully assembled, and drive activity will be indicated by the LED on the computer control panel.

3. The drive may be installed in any free bay. The left-hand bay (if there is one) is often the most convenient from the point of view of providing easy access to the connectors at the back of the drive. If the hard drive is located below the floppy drive(s), the connectors may be difficult to reach in the restricted space created by the relative positions of the drive(s) and the power supply. Secure the drive in position with drive clamps. (A few double-ended clamps are usually supplied, and these are needed to clamp the inside rails when a hard and a floppy drive are positioned horizontally, next to each other).

4. Connect a 4-pin power cable to the drive, then interface an IDE 40-pin hard drive ribbon cable from the drive to the controller card, bearing in mind that the color-coded side of the cable should align with pin #1 (or the lowest numbered pin if the count does not start at 1). (See Figures 4-11 and 4-14 in Section 4.)

5. If you did not install a composite IDE controller and multi-I/O card during original assembly, now is a good time to install a plain multi-I/O card. Install it in any convenient slot in the same manner as you installed other cards, then make the ribbon cable connections from the loose end plate and install the end plate next to the I/O card.

6. Insert the DOS boot disk into drive A and boot the computer. It will again be necessary to enter the setup program in order to record details of the hard disk drive.

Section 9

Setting Up a Hard Disk

Initializing a Non-IDE Hard Disk Drive

If you have a non-IDE hard disk drive that must be initialized (low-level formatted) before formatting, you will need to use one of the following programs:

- Programs supplied with the hard disk drive
- Proprietary programs (Speedstor is an example)
- Programs built into the BIOS setup utility
- The DOS DEBUG program

For the first two, floppy disks with user instructions are provided, and the reader should follow the instructions. (Most computer stores carry proprietary initializing programs.)

If there is an initializing program in the setup utility, the reader should simply follow instructions after invoking setup.

The DOS DEBUG program can only be used for initializing when the actual initializing program is resident in a BIOS chip on the hard disk controller card. Not all cards have such a program. However, RLL cards generally do. Again, follow the instructions provided with the card.

CAUTION
Hard disks with an IDE interface are pre-initialized, and any attempt to initialize again may destroy the disk.

Formatting a Hard Disk

1. With the computer running and the DOS boot disk in the A drive, at the A> prompt type **FDISK** and **<Enter>**. In addition to a descriptive heading, the following will appear on the screen:

   1. Create DOS partition or logical DOS drive
   2. Set active partition
   3. Delete DOS partition or logical DOS drive
   4. Display partition data

   Enter choice: [1]

Tip A DOS partition provides space for the operating system as well as for user programs and data. Because a hard disk can hold more than one type of operating system at the same time, more than one partition can be created if needed.

2. Since you need to create a single DOS partition, **<Enter>** to select Choice 1 and to cause the next screen to appear:

   1. Create primary DOS partition
   2. Create extended DOS partition
   3. Create logical DOS drive(s) in the extended DOS partition

   Enter choice: [1]

3. You need to create a primary partition, therefore **<Enter>** to select Choice 1 and to cause the next screen to appear:

   System will now restart
   Insert DOS diskette in drive A:
   Press any key when ready...

4. Press any key and your PC will reboot automatically.

5. After the system has rebooted on the floppy disk, bypass the time and date and type **Format c: /s** and **<Enter>**. The screen will now display:

   WARNING. ALL DATA ON
   NON-REMOVABLE DISK
   DRIVE C: WILL BE LOST!
   Proceed with Format (Y/N)?

Tip The /s is a switch command which tells the DOS FORMAT program to also transfer the system files from the floppy to the hard disk, thereby making the hard disk bootable—see the following note.

NOTE

The system files are IO.SYS, MSDOS.SYS, and COMMAND.COM. The first two are hidden files—that is, they are not seen when a directory of files on a disk is requested. If they are not present on a boot disk the boot will fail, resulting in the message:

Non-System disk or disk error
Replace and strike any key when ready

In addition, if DOS cannot find the COMMAND.COM file, the following message will be displayed:

Bad or missing Command Interpreter

6. Type **Y** and **<Enter>** to cause the DOS FORMAT program on the DOS floppy disk to format the hard drive which is designated "C." The percentage of format completed will be displayed until 100% is reached when the **Format complete** message will appear and, after a pause, **System transferred** followed by **Volume label (11 characters, Enter for none)?**

Tip All disks can be labeled, as volumes of books can be named, and DOS allows up to 11 characters for this name.

7. If a volume label is desired, type in the chosen name at this point and then **<Enter>**, otherwise just **<Enter>**. Next, the following will appear with the x's shown on this page representing actual numbers on the screen: numbers that will vary according to disk size.

xxxxxxx	**bytes total disk space**
xxxx	**bytes used by system**
xxx	**bytes in bad sectors**
xxxxxxx	**bytes available on disk**
xxx	**bytes in each allocation unit**
xxx	**allocation units available on disk**

Volume Serial Number is xxx xxx

Tip Disks that hold the system files are given a serial number by DOS.

8. Remove the boot disk from drive A and reboot the computer from the hard disk by pressing **Ctrl+Alt+Del**.

Directories and Files

If DOS directory and file structures are new to the reader, the following summary may be found useful; otherwise proceed to "Loading the DOS Files." This summary includes hands-on practice at making directories, and in order to clarify the exercise a command needs to be loaded into RAM. The command, which is PG, causes the active directory to be included in the drive prompt. At this time we do not have any directories, so that when you execute this command the C> will simply change to C:\> with the backslash indicating the current directory, in this case the root directory.

1. Type the command **PROMPT PG** and **<Enter>**. Observe the change to the prompt.

DOS organizes files on a hard disk to make them easy to find just as files in a good filing cabinet system can be found. The file storage system, shown in Figure 9-1, is broken down as follows:

> First level - Files and/or Directories
> Second level - Files and/or Subdirectories
> Third level - Files and/or Sub-subdirectories

The directory structure can continue with ever-growing subdirectories, although this can become cumbersome and it is usually better to split the subject at the directory level. For example, instead of a single STAFF directory, use STAFF-OFFICE and STAFF-PLANT directories, under which further subdirectories can be made.

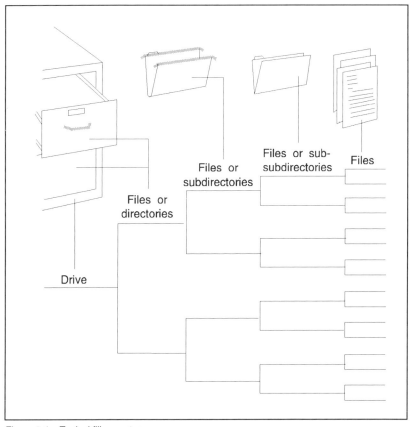

Figure 9-1   Typical filing system

A directory can be created on a floppy or hard disk drive, and it is made at the root prompt. A directory is made by typing MD (MD means "make directory") followed by a space and then the name of the directory which may not consist of more than eight characters. To make a directory on the hard disk perform the following steps.

1. To make a STAFF directory from the C:\> prompt, type **MD STAFF** and **<Enter>**. Log or "change" to that directory from the C:\> prompt by typing **CD\STAFF** and **<Enter>**. The prompt should now read C:\STAFF>.

2. Make a FIELD subdirectory from the C:\STAFF> prompt by typing **MD FIELD** and **<Enter>**, then enter that directory by typing **CD FIELD** and **<Enter>**.

91

NOTE

When moving from a directory to a subdirectory, a space must be substituted for the backslash. However, if the move is from C:\> to the FIELD subdirectory, then the command would be CD\STAFF\FIELD.

A directory (or subdirectory) may be removed, but it must be empty of files. The command is best given at the level above the subdirectory to be removed, although it can be made from C root by including the full path in the command.

3. Remove the FIELD subdirectory at the C:\STAFF> prompt by typing **CD** and **<Enter>** followed by **RD FIELD** and **<Enter>** (RD means "remove directory"). Next, change to the C:\> prompt and remove the STAFF directory by typing **RD STAFF** and **<Enter>**.

A file can be created from the keyboard at any prompt using the COPY CON command, although most files are created automatically from within application programs when text or data needs to be saved. A file name may not consist of more than eight characters, and there are some DOS restricted characters such as * and : and ; (for a full list, refer to your DOS manual). File names are usually followed by a period and a three-letter extension such as .SYS for system, or .EXE for executable. Application programs such as word processors, databases, and graphics, usually append their own extension automatically.

A file may be deleted by typing DEL followed by filename and extension, and then **<Enter>**. However, it is necessary to be in the directory where the file resides, unless the path is included with the filename.

Loading the DOS Files

Although at this stage the computer has booted off the hard disk because the system files are there, it will have very limited capabilities. The first step to improve the situation is to create a DOS directory on the computer's hard disk to hold all the DOS files that are on the DOS floppy disks. To do this, perform the steps that follow unless the version of DOS you are using dictates a different procedure. (Read the appropriate part of your DOS user manual.)

1. At the C:\> prompt type **MD DOS** and **<Enter>**. Next, type **CD\DOS** and **<Enter>** to enter the new DOS directory.

2. Place the first DOS disk into the A drive and type at the C:\> prompt **COPY A:*.*** and **<Enter>**. (An asterisk is a DOS wild card thus, in essence, the command means "regardless of name and extension, copy to C:\> all files that are on the disk in drive A.")

As the files are copied they will be displayed by name on the screen, and when they are all copied the screen will display the number of files copied.

3. Repeat step 3 until all the DOS floppy disks have been copied to the hard disk.

Creating the CONFIG.SYS File

The CONFIG.SYS (configuration system) file instructs DOS on how to configure the operating system when the computer is booted. The size of this file depends largely on the number and complexity of the application programs to be run. It loads device drivers, sets the number of DOS buffers, specifies the number of file handles, and more.

A device driver is a memory resident program required by DOS for devices that DOS does not recognize automatically, such as mice or extended memory. A buffer is a segment of memory that temporarily stores data while it is being transferred from one device to another. File handles control the number of files DOS can have open at one time.

Files may be created from the keyboard (console) by using the DOS COPY CON command.

1. To make a CONFIG.SYS file containing FILES and BUFFER commands and type:

   CD\ <Enter>
   COPY CON CONFIG.SYS <Enter>
   BUFFERS=15 <Enter>
   FILES=15 <Enter>
   <F6> <Enter>

The CD\ command changes the directory from DOS, which was the active directory, to C root, which is where the new file must reside. The

F6 command (or alternatively the key combination Ctrl+Z may be used) creates a ^Z (end-of-file marker) to which DOS responds with **1 File(s) copied**.

Creating the AUTOEXEC.BAT File

The AUTOEXEC.BAT (automatic execution batch) file executes a series of DOS commands each time the system is booted in order to save the user from having to type them in each time. Two such commands that are very useful are PG, which you have already experienced, and PATH.

In most cases DOS is unable to leapfrog from one directory to another in search of a file. PATH specifies names of directories enabling DOS to search in those directories. For example, if a DOS command is typed at the C:\> prompt with the DOS directory not in the path, the screen response will be **Bad command or file name**, and to execute the command the user must change to the DOS directory and repeat the command.

1. Make an AUTOEXEC.BAT file for your system by typing the following:

   CD\ <Enter>
   COPY CON AUTOEXEC.BAT <Enter>
   ECHO OFF <Enter>
   CLS <Enter>
   PROMPT PG <Enter>
   PATH C:\;C:\DOS <Enter>
   <F6> <Enter>

The DOS ECHO OFF inhibits the display of DOS command names. CLS erases the contents of the screen. With the PATH command, entries must be exactly as shown, and if new directories are subsequently added, their exact name must be preceded by ;C:\ with no spaces. F6 causes DOS to respond with **1 File(s) copied**.

For a detailed explanation of the ECHO command and others that are difficult to understand, refer to your DOS user manual.

2. Reboot the computer by pressing **Ctrl+Alt+Del** to make the changes effective and to ensure that the computer will boot off the hard drive.

NOTE

When either the CONFIG.SYS or the AUTOEXEC.BAT files are first created, or at any subsequent time when they are edited, the computer must be rebooted to make the files or the changes become effective. The warm boot carried out by pressing Ctrl+Alt+Delete is acceptable, as is also the cold boot achieved by either pressing the Reset button on the computer control panel or by switching the machine off and on. In the latter case, wait for 30 seconds before switching on again to allow electrical current to drain from all electrical devices in the computer.

Formatting and Copying Floppy Disks

Formatting Floppy Disks

DOS versions 5.0 and later offer a number of floppy disk formatting options. The options, also known as "switches," must be typed in the correct format which, following the basic command, always commences with a space followed by a backslash. The basic command is Format x: where x is the drive letter. The main switches with explanations follow.

Format x:	Formats a floppy disk to either 1.2MB or 1.44MB depending on the size of the drive
Format x: /4	Formats a 1.2MB disk to 360K
Format x: /F:720	Formats a 1.44MB disk to 720K

To quick-format a disk, add a space and /Q at the end of the format instruction.

To make a disk bootable, add a space and /S at the end of the format instruction, which commands DOS to transfer a copy of the system files to the disk.

1. For practice, insert a new high-density disk in the appropriate floppy disk drive, and at the C:\> prompt type **Format x:** (where x is the drive designation A or B).

2. Execute the format command by pressing **Enter** and the screen will display the following:

> **Insert new diskette for drive x**
> **and press ENTER when ready...**

3. Press **Enter** and disk formatting will commence with the percentage completed displayed until 100% is reached; then the message **Format complete** will appear, followed by:

Volume label (11 characters, ENTER for none)?

Each disk can be labeled, as volumes of books can be named, and DOS allows up to 11 characters for this name.

4. If a volume label is desired, type in the chosen name at this point and then **<Enter>**, otherwise just **<Enter>**. Next, the following will appear with the x's shown in this book representing actual numbers on the screen, numbers that will vary according to disk size.

xxxxxxx	**bytes total disk space**
xxxx	**bytes used by system**
xxx	**bytes in bad sectors**
xxxxxxx	**bytes available on disk**
xxx	**bytes in each allocation unit**
xxx	**allocation units available on disk**

NOTE

Only disks that hold the system files will be given a serial number by DOS.

5. The screen will display the message **Format another (Y/N)?** Type **Y** to have the full procedure repeated or **N** to close the program.

Making Copies of Floppy Disks

Disks can fail! Therefore, working copies should be made of all application program disks for storage in a safe place with the originals.

A disk (the source disk) is copied by reading its contents into RAM, removing it, and inserting a blank formatted floppy (the target disk) onto which the files being held in memory can be copied. However, one of the vagaries of DOS is that you are unable to address more than the first 640K of RAM, some of which is being used by system files. (If necessary, refer back to Section 3 and Figure 3-6 to refresh your memory on this subject.) As a result, DOS copies 1.2MB and 1.44MB floppy disks in several increments of up to 576K at a time.

There are two DOS copy commands. The first is DISKCOPY, which is the most efficient but can only be used when copying from and to the same media (e.g., 1.2MB to 1.2MB). When copying from dissimilar media, XCOPY is the DOS command that is used. However, XCOPY does not write over any existing files that might be on the target disk, whereas DISKCOPY does, and XCOPY cannot be used in a single disk system, unless you first copy the files to a temporary directory on the hard disk and thence to the new floppy.

Perform the following steps to copy floppy disks on a system with a single or two dissimilar floppy drives using the DISKCOPY command.

1. Type **DISKCOPY A: A:** then **<Enter>** and the screen will display:

    Insert SOURCE diskette in drive A:

    Press any key to continue...
    Copying xx tracks
    yy Sectors/Track, 2 Side (s)

    xx will be 40 for a 360K disk and 80 for the 720K, the 1.2MB, and the 1.44MB. yy will be 9 for the 360K and the 720K, 15 for the 1.2MB, and 18 for the 1.44MB.

2. Insert a disk with data on it and then press any key to commence copying the disk into RAM and then to display the following message:

    Insert TARGET diskette in Drive A:

    Press any key to continue...

3. Remove the source disk and insert a blank, formatted disk, then press any key.

This sequence of inserting source and target disks will be repeated (if necessary) until all the data has been copied and then the screen will display:

    Copy another diskette (Y/N?)

4. Type **Y** and **<Enter>** to cause the whole process to be repeated with a new disk, or type **N** and **<Enter>** to terminate the program.

To use the XCOPY command on a system with a 3.5-inch and a 5.25-inch floppy disk drive, perform the following steps.

1. Insert a disk containing data into drive A and a blank, formatted disk into drive B.

2. Type **XCOPY A:*.* B: /S** where *.* means all files on the disk, and /S means include any subdirectories (DISKCOPY automatically copies subdirectories). Press **Enter** and the response is **Reading source file(s)**; this is followed by a list of all the files as they are copied, and the cursor finishes up at the drive prompt. No further action is necessary.

Tip You can XCOPY files from any disk to any other disk.

Section 11

Software Programs

Microsoft Windows

As with most modern software programs, installing Microsoft Windows involves no more than inserting the first disk into drive A, typing SETUP, and pressing Enter. Windows will then painlessly install itself, requesting more disks, asking an occasional question, and requiring you to make a few simple choices. Setting up the Program Manager after the program is installed may present a little more difficulty, but the user manual will guide you.

Any application program you install that runs under Windows also installs relatively easily. When you load Windows, you set the scene for the other programs by providing specifications for peripherals such as your printer. Once such information is recorded by Windows it appears automatically in the other applications. Similarly, any fonts you install in Windows become available to the other programs.

With Windows, you can choose to have your PC boot right into Windows, seemingly cutting out DOS. Then you can run any program from the Windows Program Manager, including those that are not true Windows applications. With Windows you can also have more than one application running at the same time, but if you wish to exploit this capability you will require plenty of RAM.

You load applications that run under Windows from within the Program Manager, and the files are copied from the floppy disks automatically to directories set up automatically. For a good understanding of Windows, read *Learn Windows in a Day*, also available from Wordware Publishing, Inc.

Application Programs

When you load software application programs that do not run under Windows, directories may need to be set up, and entries may have to be made in either the CONFIG.SYS file or the AUTOEXEC.BAT or both. Frequently, the software will do this automatically, but on other occasions the installation instructions will direct the user to do it manually using either the DOS editor (Edit), the DOS line editor (Edlin), or a word processing program (in which case the file must be saved as an unformatted or ASCII file).

You load non-Windows application program files into a directory either automatically or manually, just as you did with the DOS files. Some programs leave you to create the directory while others do it automatically. If the latter case, if you have already created a directory, higher-end programs see it and do not create another one, but less sophisticated programs may blindly go ahead and you finish up with two directories, one of which (the empty one) you will need to remove. Worse, some of the low-end programs make a subdirectory under your directory, making access to the program difficult and, again, this surplus directory must be removed.

User manuals supplied with software application programs give detailed loading procedures and most of them are easy to follow, requiring you to simply type **INSTALL <Enter>** and then follow screen instructions. However, sometimes the skills of the program's software writers exceed those of the manual author, and the manual may be difficult to understand. Whenever possible, follow the manual's loading instructions, and only as a last resort try the following.

Generally speaking, the first of an application program's disks has the Install file which, once executed, takes you to the screen instructions for the installation process. The Install file will usually have the extension .EXE or .COM, and to find it, place the first floppy disk into drive A and type **DIR A:*.EXE <Enter>**, which will display all files on the disk with an .EXE extension. If INSTALL.EXE is displayed, simply type **INSTALL <Enter>** and follow instructions. If it does not display, try repeating the procedure using *.COM instead of *.EXE.

Some application programs require entries to be made in either the CONFIG.SYS file or the AUTOEXEC.BAT file, or both. Frequently, the software will do this automatically, but on occasions the installation instructions will direct the user to do it manually, as described above.

Automatic additions to the CONFIG.SYS and the AUTOEXEC.BAT files sometimes interfere with existing commands in those files. Consequently, it is good practice to carefully view those files in any program that will display them, making alterations if necessary and remembering to reboot your computer to make the alterations effective.

Section 12

Microsoft DOS for Beginners

Introduction

Overview

Microsoft DOS is the disk operating system for the IBM PC-compatible. Originally released in 1981 with IBM's first personal computer as PC-DOS, DOS has become a standard for microcomputer operating systems.

Operating System

An operating system provides an interface between the user and the computer and is essential for normal computer operations and for managing such system resources as disks, printers, and other peripheral devices. Furthermore, DOS permits the execution of other programs such as word processing and database applications.

Users see DOS in different ways. To some it is no more than a command processor that executes the commands the user types on the keyboard. Others who work from within Windows are seldom aware of DOS; and for systems programmers, DOS is a low-level interface to disk, directory, file, and program control functions.

Early versions of DOS suffered severe limitations such as being able to only recognize a maximum of 32 megabytes at a time on a hard disk drive, making it necessary to divide larger hard disks into several drives such as C, D, E, etc. Later versions showed improvement but remained limited in their handling of RAM. With versions 5.0 and better, many limitations were removed, and with 6.0 and better came such sophistication as disk doubling.

Using DOS

Loading

When a computer is booted (switched on), built-in routines prepare the system to accept DOS. Details of the computer's BIOS (Basic Input/Output System) are displayed on the monitor, then the routines look at drive A to see if DOS is waiting to be loaded, and if DOS is not there the BIOS will look for it at other installed drives. If DOS is not found, either a cursor will blink under the last displayed line on the monitor until DOS is provided, or a message will be displayed asking for a DOS disk.

If a hard disk (usually drive C) is not installed, insert a DOS boot disk in drive A prior to booting so that when the BIOS looks at drive A it will find DOS, activate the disk drive, and read DOS into memory.

If a hard disk containing DOS is installed, it is not necessary to insert a DOS boot disk, since the BIOS will pass over drive A and find DOS when it looks at drive C.

If a computer is booted off a floppy DOS disk, the monitor will display the following request for the date when DOS has loaded:

Current date is Fri 11-23-1995
Enter new date (mm-dd-yy):

The displayed current date is unlikely to be correct; thus, if the date will be needed for use with application programs, type the correct date in accordance with the format displayed and press **Enter**. The next message appears:

Current time is 17:21:04
Enter new time:

The displayed current time is also unlikely to be correct, in which case type the correct time in the required format and press Enter. This will lead to the DOS prompt of the current drive. DOS is now loaded. (If there is no requirement for the correct date and time, press Enter at each message to reach the prompt.)

To change from the current drive to, for example, drive B, type **B:**, then **<Enter>** and the prompt will change to B>.

The Keyboard

If you press and hold down any of the white keys (with the exception of white function keys), the character, number, or symbol will repeat until the key is released. Therefore, keys should be pressed sharply, or clicked, rather than pressed slowly.

Keys that are different from those of a regular typewriter have specific DOS functions. For example:

Shift These keys shift the alphabetical keys to uppercase, and numeric or symbol keys to the symbol shown at the top of each key.

Caps Lock As the name suggests, this key locks the Shift function until pressed again, but it does not affect any of the numeric or symbol keys.

Esc In DOS, the Escape key will nullify a line of type but will leave it displayed with a slash at the end of it and the cursor will move to the next line. In application programs it has other uses.

Ctrl The Control key only functions when used in conjunction with certain other keys.

Num Lock The Numeric Lock key changes the cursor movement keys at the right of the board to a numeric function.

Break The Break key, located on the front face of the Pause or Scroll Lock keys, is used in conjunction with the Ctrl key to cancel a command.

Print Screen Sometimes displayed as PrtSc, this key is used with a Shift key or the Ctrl key. Holding down a Shift key and pressing the Print Screen key will cause the contents of the screen to be printed. Holding down the Ctrl key and pressing the Print Screen key causes each line to be printed as it is typed. Using the sequence a second time will stop the printing function.

NOTE

To Print Screen on some laser printers, after pressing Enter you may need to take the printer off line and press the Form Feed button to force the page to print.

Key Combinations

For certain commands it is necessary to type the DOS codes, and for others DOS requires some keys to be held down while others are pressed. The following is a list of such commands that are used frequently. Keys that are held down are followed by the + sign.

CLS   Type **CLS** and **<Enter>** to clear the screen of all type.

Ctrl and **Num Lock**   Press **Ctrl+Num Lock**, or **Ctrl+S** to stop text scrolling on the screen. Press any key to allow scrolling to resume.

Ctrl, **Alt**, and **Delete**   Press **Ctrl+Alt+Delete** to cause the system to reboot. This is known as a warm boot, as opposed to a cold boot caused by pressing the Reset button or by turning the main switch off and on. (If cold booting a computer from the main switch, it should be left off for at least 30 seconds to allow electrical charges on chips, transistors, and other devices to disperse.)

DOS Files

Information that you enter (type) into the computer's volatile memory must be saved before the computer is powered down. Volatile memory is like the memory of a human: it is only available while the computer is alive. Power down (kill the computer), and the memory disappears until the computer is booted again but, unfortunately, nothing is remembered. Saving data is achieved by storing it in a file on a disk. When the file is required again, DOS can be made to read the disk and display the file on screen.

Text files contain readable data, while command files contain instructions DOS needs to carry out commands.

All files must have a filename which can be up to eight characters long with no spaces or punctuation marks. Filenames may have extensions consisting of three characters separated from the name by a period but with no spaces.

If DOS is requested to find and display a file, it will only look in the active drive unless a different drive is specified. The command to display a file on screen in DOS is TYPE. To display the file MEMO.TXT stored on a floppy disk in drive A, from active drive C, type **TYPE A:MEMO.TXT**, then **<Enter>**.

The drive, directory [if any], filename, and extension are known as the file specification. Also note that DOS is not case-sensitive.

DOS File Commands

Directory (DIR)

Directories can be created in DOS for storing files. For example, to create the directory STAFF in the active drive, type **MKDIR STAFF**, then **<Enter>**. (The simple form MD can also be used.)

To change into the STAFF directory from the active drive, type **CHDIR STAFF**, then **<Enter>**. (The simple form CD can also be used.)

Subdirectories can be made within directories by using the same command when in the parent directory.

Unfortunately, DOS does not automatically indicate which directory has been selected unless an additional command is given. To enter that command type **PROMPT PG**, then **<Enter>**. When the command is put into the system, either from the keyboard or by adding it into the boot procedure, the result is to display the directory name after the prompt. For example, C:\STAFF>. The backslash is a DOS indication that the name which follows the prompt is that of a directory. To view the contents of the STAFF directory when at the C:\STAFF> prompt, type **DIR**, then **<Enter>**, or from the C:\> root prompt, type **DIR C:\STAFF**, then **<Enter>**.

DOS "Wild Card" Characters

These characters are * and ? and are useful for activities with groups of files. The * can represent all eight characters in a filename or the extension letters. For example, to see only those files in a directory with the file extension DOC, type **DIR *.DOC**, then **<Enter>**. The ? represents only a single character; thus, to achieve the same result, type **DIR ????????.DOC**, then **<Enter>**. In either case, DOS would list all files within the directory that have the extension DOC.

COPY

The DOS COPY command allows files to be copied from one part of a disk to another (for example, from one directory to another) or from one disk to another disk. To copy to the C root a file we will call PAYRATES.TXT which resides in the STAFF directory, from the C:\STAFF> prompt, type **COPY PAYRATES.TXT C:**, then **<Enter>**.

If another directory exists called ACCOUNTS, to copy the file to it from the STAFF directory, type **COPY PAYRATES.TXT C:\ACCOUNTS**, then **<Enter>**.

To copy the same file from the STAFF directory to the ACCOUNTS directory when in C root, type **COPY C:\STAFF\PAYRATES.TXT C:\ACCOUNTS**, then **<Enter>**.

When copying from disk to disk, the commands are basically the same but with the other drive letter used. For example, when in the STAFF directory, to copy the PAYRATES file to a floppy disk in drive A, type **COPY PAYRATES.TXT A:**, then **<Enter>**, or from the A:\> prompt, type **COPY C:\STAFF\PAYRATES.TXT**, then **<Enter>**.

COPY CON

This command allows a file to be created (in both name and content) directly from the keyboard (console). However, most files are created automatically by application programs, thus COPY CON is used mainly for creating batch files which are discussed later in this section.

To create a file in the STAFF directory called PAYRATES.TXT containing the message "Overtime will be time and a half," at the C:\> prompt type **COPY CON C:\PAYRATES.TXT**, then **<Enter>**, and on the next line, "Overtime will be time and a half" followed by **<Enter>**, and on the next line, press **Ctrl + Z** or **F6**, which will cause ^Z to be displayed, then **<Enter>** again and DOS will acknowledge with the message:

1 File(s) copied

TYPE

This command causes the contents of a file to be displayed on the screen. If in the STAFF directory, to display the contents of the file just created, type **TYPE PAYRATES.TXT**, then **<Enter>**. If at the C:\> prompt, type **TYPE C:\STAFF\PAYRATES.TXT**, then **<Enter>**.

RENAME (REN)

This command allows a file to be renamed or moved. To rename the file PAYRATES.TXT to RATESPAY.TXT when in the STAFF directory, type **REN PAYRATES.TXT RATESPAY.TXT** then **<Enter>**, or from C root type **REN C:\STAFF\PAYRATES.TXT C:\STAFF\RATESPAY.TXT**, then **<Enter>**.

To move the file to the ACCOUNTS directory when in the STAFF directory, type **REN PAYRATES.TXT C:\ACCOUNTS\ PAYRATES.TXT**, then **<Enter>**, or from C root type **REN C:\STAFF\PAYRATES.TXT C:\ACCOUNTS\PAYRATES.TXT**, then **<Enter>**.

Managing Disks

Volume Label

A disk may be given a name (volume label) to identify its contents. With the drive selected for the target disk, type **VOL**, then **<Enter>** to view the name (if any) of the disk. The name can be up to 11 characters and one space long, and it can be added to a disk, or changed, by typing **LABEL**, pressing **Enter** and then following instructions.

When the directory of a disk is displayed using the DIR command, the volume label (if any) will be displayed first. When copying application program disks (including DOS), their volume labels will also be copied.

Formatting

The surface of a disk needs to be organized before it can receive data; this is called formatting. To format a floppy disk on a system fitted with a fixed disk, type **FORMAT A:** and **<Enter>**. After following screen prompts to insert the disk to be formatted and to <Enter>, DOS will indicate that it is formatting and, when complete, will display Volume label (11 characters, ENTER for none)? Either type in the name and **<Enter>** or just **<Enter>** if a name is not wanted. Complete formatting instructions for floppy disks are given in Section 10 and for hard disks in Section 9.

Making a System Disk

A system disk is another name for a boot disk: a formatted disk that contains three DOS files: two hidden files and the COMMAND.COM file. The hidden files (MSDOS.SYS and IO.SYS) create what is known as the first and second layers of the boot and are no longer used once the system has booted. The COMMAND.COM file remains active in RAM. To create a system disk, the three files must be transferred from a DOS disk, or the disk must be formatted as a boot disk when the files are transferred automatically. The system files can be transferred from any drive that holds them by typing **SYS** when in that drive, followed by the letter of the drive (plus a colon) where the target disk is. For example, **A:>SYS B: or C:\DOS>SYS A:** and then **<Enter>**. System or bootable disks were covered in Section 10.

Copying Disks

The DOS DISKCOPY command makes an exact copy of a disk and will wipe out any files already on the target disk. Copying disks was covered in Section 10.

Deleting Files

A file may be deleted by using the DEL command preceding the filename. For example, **DEL C:\ACCOUNTS\PAYRATES.TXT** and then **<Enter>**.

Checking Disks

The DOS check disk command, CHKDSK, will check out the files and directories on a disk and display an analysis of them as well as the size of the computer's memory and the remaining free bytes on the disk. To have the active disk checked, the command is **CHKDSK** and then **<Enter>**. Or to have a different disk checked (for example, checking the A drive from the C drive), **CHKDSK A:** and then **<Enter>**.

Heavy or careless usage of a disk, particularly when using certain application programs, can cause clusters of data to be lost. In such a case, when the disk is checked, DOS will first advise that a number of clusters have been found in certain "chains," and then ask if they should be converted to files. If Y is pressed, DOS will attempt conversion and the files will show up in root as FILE0000.CHK for the first, FILE0001.CHK for the next, and so on. These files can be displayed using the TYPE command and retained by renaming if wanted or discarded by deleting.

If N is pressed, DOS proceeds to check the disk and the lost clusters remain, using disk space.

If the switch /F (for fix) is used after the CHKDSK command, DOS will display the same choices, but if N is pressed, the lost clusters are automatically deleted and space is freed up on the disk.

Directory Tree

This command will display all the directories that have been created. Based on the previous examples, if a PAY subdirectory is created under STAFF, and PAYABLE and RECEIVE directories under ACCOUNTS, typing TREE will display the schematics shown in the following figure.

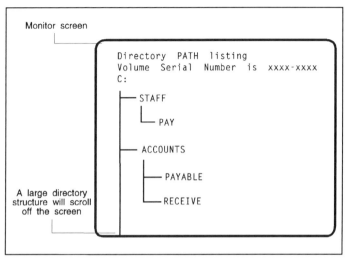

Figure 12-1   The DOS tree

PATH Command

The path is the route taken by DOS to seek a file. Unless a path is defined in an AUTOEXEC.BAT file in the boot drive, DOS will only be able to search the drive that is active. For example, if there is no path specified and CHKDSK is ordered when in the STAFF directory, DOS will be unable to execute the command because it will be unable to track from the STAFF directory to the DOS directory where the file CHKDSK.COM resides.

Batch Files

A batch file is a text file that contains DOS commands and is used to automate frequently used commands. The AUTOEXEC.BAT file described in the following paragraph is an excellent example.

111

AUTOEXEC.BAT

This batch file is placed in C root so that during the boot DOS looks at it and carries out any commands it contains. The PG command previously discussed in this section is an example of a command that goes into the AUTOEXEC.BAT. This file can be created by using the COPY CON command, or it can be edited in the DOS editor or a word processing program. If the latter is used, the file should be saved as an unformatted file.

The DOS Manual

As you gain more experience, read in greater depth the DOS manual supplied with your DOS disks in order to become familiar with more advanced features. For ease of learning, study *Learn DOS 6.2 in a Day*, another book from Wordware Publishing, Inc.

Glossary

8-bit	Limits data path on a bus or adapter card to a width of 8 bits.
10-pin ribbon cable	Cable that connects ports to an I/O card.
16-bit	Limits data path on a bus or adapter card to a width of 16 bits.
20-pin ribbon cable	Hard drive data cable.
32-bit	Limits data path on a bus or adapter card to a width of 32 bits.
34-pin ribbon cable	Hard or floppy drive controller cable.
386-enhanced mode	Creates "virtual" memory when used with 80386 CPUs and higher, and appropriate software.
40-pin ribbon cable	IDE hard drive controller cable
Adapter card	A printed circuit card, or board, used to control and connect electronic devices to the motherboard.
Address	Location in memory for the storage of specific information.
Address bus	The wire path that carries addressing information to specify a location for data in memory.
Asyn 1 and Asyn 2	Asynchronous (as opposed to synchronized) communication ports.
Auto-parking	A technique on modern hard disk drives to prevent the read/write heads touching the platters when a PC is not operating.
Back up	To copy data from one disk to another (or tape) as a safeguard in case the first disk loses its data.
Bare-bones	A partially built PC consisting of case, power supply, and motherboard.
Base plate	The bottom of a PC's case.
Battery	Maintains the configuration information in the CMOS chip in an AT when the PC is switched off.

Baud	Measurement of transmission speed for a modem and other devices. One bit per second equals one baud.
Bay	Receptacle in a PC for a disk drive.
Beep-code	Translation of the speaker signals transmitted by the BIOS.
Binary system	The counting system used by CPUs based on the numbers 0 and 1.
BIOS	Basic Input/Output System. Preprogrammed instructions that allow a PC to start operating when switched on.
Bit	The binary counting unit.
Boot record	Starts the DOS boot process and defines disk characteristics.
Booting	The loading of the stages of DOS.
Bootstrap program	The program that starts the boot process.
Bus	Electrical interface between motherboard and adapter cards.
Bus-mouse	A mouse with its own adapter card.
Byte	Eight bits.
Cache	A cache of high speed memory, in addition to RAM, which can be used for fast data transfer.
CAD	Computer Aided Design. Application software specifically for design creation such as architectural or engineering drawings.
Cap	The shorting (switch) unit that "caps" jumper pins.
Capacitor	An electrical device that develops and holds a charge of electricity.
CHKDSK	DOS command that checks and reports on the condition of a disk.
Clock speed	The speed of the CPU in megahertz.
Clone	A copy of an IBM PC.
Cluster	A set of contiguous sectors on a disk.
CMOS	Complimentary Metal Oxide Semiconductor. A programmable chip for storing an AT's configuration.

COM1 or COM2	Communications ports 1 and 2. Also called serial ports.
COMMAND.COM	DOS command processor that executes internal and external commands.
COMMSPEC	A command telling DOS to find the COMMAND.COM file under a different name.
Compress	1. A technique for compressing files so that they occupy less space. 2. A technique for defragmenting a disk.
CONFIG.SYS	A user-defined DOS system file that configures a PC's system.
Conflict	An error that occurs when two devices attempt to use the same system resources.
Connector	A "plug" on the end of a cable.
Control-panel	A switch panel with LED lights on the face of a PC used for controlling some features and indicating activity of others.
Controller	An adapter card that controls disk drives. Also used in the term "video controller."
Conventional memory	The first 640 kilobytes of RAM memory.
CPU	Central Processing Unit. The CPU is, in effect, the actual computing device in a PC.
Cross-linked files	Files with confused pointers which inhibit DOS from accessing them.
Cylinder	Tracks of the same DOS number on each hard disk platter.
Data bus	The path along which data is carried; eight bits at a time in an 8-bit bus, 16 bits in a 16-bit bus, etc.
Data encoding scheme	The formula used by a hard disk drive controller to define how a hard disk will read, write, and store data.
DEBUG	A DOS programming utility also used in conjunction with qualifiers for other activities such as XT hard disk initializing.
Device driver	A program that controls a device; a mouse for example.

Diagnostic program	1. A resident program in the BIOS that carries out self-diagnostics. 2. An application program for diagnosing faults.
Digitizing tablet	An input device consisting of a stylus and a sensitized board.
DIP chip	Dual Inline Package. The original type of memory chip that inserts into rows (banks) of sockets.
Dipswitches	Mini-switches used to set parameters.
Disk crash	When the read/write heads of a hard disk are jarred into striking the platters.
Disk fragmentation	The separation of a file on a disk into several non-contiguous parts as a result of editing.
DMA channel	Direct Memory Access. A fast route for bypassing the CPU in the transfer of information when CPU involvement is not required.
DOS	Disk Operating System. A software interface between PC and user.
DOS kernel	The portion of DOS responsible for directory and file management, and for interfacing with applications.
DOS sectors	Part of a track on a disk.
Dot pitch	The combined size of the red, green, and blue phosphor spots on the back of a monitor's screen stated in millimeters.
Dot-matrix printer	A printer that creates images by striking an inked tape with varying numbers of pins.
DPI	Dots Per Inch. The number of dots in one square inch; used to specify screen, printer, or scanner resolution.
DRAM	Dynamic Random Accessible Memory. Same as RAM. The volatile memory created by memory chips when a PC is switched on; used for program instruction and temporary data storage.

Drive bay	See Bay.
Drive controller	See Controller.
Drive-select jumper	Used to set numbering parameters on a disk drive.
EISA	Extended Industry Standard Architecture. A bus design compatible with ISA but incorporating many of the MCA improvements.
Error messages	Messages relayed by speaker or by screen display.
ESDI	Enhanced Small Disk Interface. A data encoding scheme for hard disk drives.
Expanded memory	Memory above 640K limited by versions of DOS preceding 5.0. See LIM.
Expansion slots	Receptacles in the bus for adapter cards.
Extended memory	Memory above 1MB in ATs not recognized by versions of DOS prior to 5.0.
FAT	File Allocation Table. Keeps track of file locations and clusters on a disk.
Formatting	Preparation of a disk to enable it to accept data.
Gigabyte (GB)	Approximately one thousand megabytes.
Graphics card	Video card that controls the display of computer generated images.
I/O address	CPU memory address for each device in a PC.
IDE	Integrated Drive Electronics. A data encoding scheme for hard disk drives.
Industry standard bus	The bus on original IBM PCs and most compatibles.
Initializing	Applying to a hard disk sets of fundamental parameters that relate to a specific type of controller.
Instruction	One step in a batch of steps that instructs the CPU to carry out a task.
Interface	Physical connection.

Interleave	An interleave number specifies how data is read or written to the sectors of a hard disk, if necessary skipping sectors in order to correlate system and disk speed.
Interrupts	A technique for putting the system on hold in order to allow another operation to take place.
Jumper	A form of switch using pins that can be shorted by a cap to make a connection.
K	Kilobyte. 1024 bytes.
LED	Light Emitting Diode. A small light used to indicate activity such as disk usage.
LIM EMS	Lotus-Intel-Microsoft Expanded Memory Specification. Allows the use of expanded memory.
Lost cluster	Inaccessible cluster caused by absence of the FAT pointer added when a file is written. Usually caused by system termination during an operation.
LPT	DOS reserved name for a parallel printer port.
Magnetic head	The read/write head on a disk drive.
MB	Megabyte. 1,048,576 bytes.
MCA	Micro Channel Architecture. An IBM bus design that uses non-standard adapter cards but offers some improvements over standard architecture.
Memory chip	An electronic device that connects to the motherboard to provide RAM when a PC is operating.
Memory map	Schematic illustration of how a PC uses memory.
Memory modes	See Real mode, Protected mode, and 386-enhanced mode.
MFM	Modified Frequency Modulation. A data encoding scheme for hard disk drives.
Mhz	Megahertz. One million cycles per second.
Micro-channel	See MCA.
Microprocessor	See CPU.

Mini tower	A half-size tower case.
MIPS	Millions of instructions per second.
Motherboard	The main board of a PC on which is housed the CPU, memory, and adapter slots, in addition to many other electronic devices.
Mouse	A peripheral device that displays a movable pointer on the monitor screen for creating graphics and activating commands.
MS-DOS	The Microsoft disk operating system.
Multi-I/O card	An adapter card providing ports such as printer, communications, and game.
Notch	An indentation on memory chips or modules and memory sockets to indicate correct installation direction.
Parallel printer port	See LPT.
Parity	A technique for checking data errors.
Path statement	An instruction that points DOS to specified directories, usually in the AUTOEXEC.BAT file.
Peripheral	Any device external to a PC.
Pixel	One illuminated dot on a monitor screen.
Platter	One of several disks that make up a hard disk drive.
Port	A connector, usually on the part of an adapter card, that is visible through the back plate of a PC.
Power supply	An internal component of a PC that steps down line power to that used by the PC.
Powering up	Switching on a PC.
Printer port	See LPT.
Protected mode	Extended memory that can be protected from interference by other memory using devices and programs.
Qualifier	An addition to a DOS command that adds to or changes the nature of the command, also known as a "switch."

Rails	Literally rails that fit to the sides of drives so that they can be slid along tracks into drive bays.
RAM	Random Accessible Memory. See DRAM.
Read/write head	See Magnetic head.
Real mode	The mode of operation of an 8088 CPU. Real mode is incorporated into 80286, 80386, and 80486 chips.
Resolution	See DPI.
Ribbon cables	Flat plastic cables with a number of embedded wires.
RLL	Run Length Limited. A data encoding scheme for hard disk drives.
ROM	Read Only Memory. Memory that has been preprogrammed and which a user can read but not write to.
SCSI	Small Computer System Interface. A data encoding scheme for hard disk drives.
Serial port	Same as COM1 or COM2.
Setup	A program in the BIOS where the PC's configuration can be entered.
SIMM	Single Inline Memory Module. See module.
Storage capacity	The number of data bytes that can be stored on a disk.
Surge protector	A device that stabilizes fluctuations in line current.
Switch	An addition to a DOS command that adds to or changes the nature of the command, also known as a "qualifier."
SX	An 80386 CPU with only a 16-bit external data path.
Terminating resister	A scheme to allow a single ribbon cable to be used with either one or two drives.
Tracks	Concentric circles on a disk for storing data.
UPS	Uninterruptible Power Supply. An external device that, in the event of a power outage, automatically supplies battery power to a PC's power supply.

VGA	Video Graphics Array. A type of color monitor.
Video card	See Adapter card and Controller card.
Video subsystem	The monitor, video card, and some internal electronics such as IRQs.
Virtual memory	Portion of unallocated hard disk space used as a form of RAM.
VRAM	Video memory
Wait-state	Delays introduced into a PC to match memory speed to hard disk speed. See also Interleave.

Index

Other Books from Wordware Publishing, Inc.

Illustrated Series
Illustrated Borland C++ 3.1
Illustrated DacEasy Accounting 4.2
Illustrated MS-DOS 5.0
Illustrated Novell NetWare
  2.x/3.x Software
Illustrated Q&A 4.0
Illustrated UNIX System V

General and Advanced Topics
111 Clipper Functions
The Complete Communications
  Handbook
Demystifying SNA
Demystifying TCP/IP
Financial Modeling using
  Lotus 1-2-3
Integrating TCP/IP into SNA
Learn P-CAD Master Designer
Mastering Magic Cards
Networking with Windows NT
Programming On-Line Help
  using C++
Understanding 3COM Networks

Hands-On Windows Programming Series
1: Intro To Window Programming
2: Child Windows
3: Painting the Screen
4: Transferring Data To and From
   Windows
5: Mouse, Timer, and Keyboard Inputs
6: Text and Special Fonts, Menus,
   and Printing

Popular Applications Series
Cost Control Using Lotus 1-2-3
Creating Help for Windows
  Applications
Desktop Publishing Handbook
Desktop Publishing with Word 2.0 for
  Windows
Desktop Publishing with WordPerfect
Desktop Publishing with WordPerfect
  for Windows

Popular App. Series (Cont.)
Developing & Distributing MS FoxPro
  2.5/2.6 for Windows Applications
Developing Utilities in Assembly
  Language
Getting the Most From Your HP
  LaserJet
HP LaserJet Handbook
Learn AmiPro in a Day (Ver 2.0 & 3.0)
Learn AutoCAD in a Day
Learn AutoCAD 12 in a Day
Learn AutoCAD LT for Windows
  in a Day
Learn C in Three Days
Learn CompuServe for Windows
  in a Day
Learn dBASE Programming in a Day
  (2nd Edition)
Learn DOS 6.0 in a Day
Learn DOS 6.2 in a Day
Learn Excel for Windows
  in a Day (Ver. 3.0 & 4.0)
Learn FoxPro 2.5 for Windows
  in a Day
Learn Freelance Graphics for
  Windows in a Day (Ver 2.0)
Learn Generic CADD 6.0 in a Day
Learn Harvard Graphics 3.0 in a Day
Learn Lotus 1-2-3 in a Day (Ver 2.0-2.4)
Learn Lotus 1-2-3 Rel. 4 for DOS
  in a Day
Learn Lotus 1-2-3 Rel. 4 for Windows
  in a Day
Learn MS Access 2.0 for Windows
  in a Day
Learn Microsoft Assembler in a Day
Learn MS Excel 5.0 for Windows
  in a Day
Learn MS FoxPro 2.5 in a Day
Learn MS PowerPoint 4.0 for
  Windows in a Day
Learn MS Publisher 2.0 for Windows
  in a Day
Learn MS Visual Basic 4.0 for
  Windows in a Day
Learn MS Word 6.0 for Windows
  in a Day

Call Wordware Publishing, Inc. for names of the bookstores in your area
(214) 423-0090

Other Books from Wordware Publishing, Inc.

Popular App. Series (Cont.)
Learn Microsoft Works in a Day
(Ver 2.0)
Learn Microsoft Works 3.0 in a Day
Learn Microsoft Works 3.0 for
Windows in a Day
Learn Norton Utilities in a Day
Learn Novell NetWare Software
in a Day
Learn OS/2 in a Day
Learn PageMaker 4.0 in a Day
Learn PageMaker 5.0 in a Day
Learn PAL in a Day
Learn PAL 4.5 in a Day
Learn Paradox 4.0 in a Day
Learn Paradox 4.5 in a Day
Learn Pascal in Three Days
Learn PC-Tools 8.0 in a Day
Learn PROCOMM PLUS 2.0 for
Widows in a Day
Learn Q&A 4.0 in a Day
Learn Quattro Pro 4.0 in a Day
Learn Quattro Pro 5.0 in a Day
Learn Quicken in a Day
Learn Timeslips for Windows
in a Day
Learn To Use Your Modem in a Day
Learn Turbo Assembler in a Day
Learn Ventura 4.0 in a Day
Learn Windows in a Day
Learn Windows NT in a Day
Learn Word 2.0 for Windows
in a Day
Learn WordPerfect in a Day
(2nd Edition)
Learn WordPerfect 5.1+ in a Day
Learn WordPerfect 6.0 in a Day
Learn WordPerfect 5.2 for Windows
in a Day
Learn WordPerfect 6.0 for Windows
in a Day
Learn WordPerfect Presentations
in a Day

Popular App. Series (Cont.)
Moving from WordPerfect for DOS to
WordPerfect for Windows
Networks for Small Businesses
Object-Oriented Programming using
Turbo C++
Programming Output Drivers using
Borland C++
Repair and Upgrade Your Own PC
WordPerfect 6.0 Survival Skills
Write TSRs Now
Write Your Own Programming
Language using C++

At A Glance Series
ACT! 2.0 for Windows at a Glance
CorelDRAW! for Windows at a Glance
CorelDRAW 5.0 for Windows
at a Glance
FoxPro at a Glance (Ver 2.5)
FoxPro 2.5 for Windows at a Glance
Lotus 1-2-3 for Windows at a Glance
Lotus 1-2-3 Rel. 4 for Windows
at a Glance
Microsoft Excel 5.0 for Windows
at a Glance
Microsoft Windows at a Glance
Microsoft Word 6.0 for Windows
at a Glance
Paradox 4.5 at a Glance
Paradox 5.0 for Windows at a Glance
Quattro Pro 5.0 at a Glance
Quattro Pro 4.0 for Windows
at a Glance
Quattro Pro 5.0 for Windows
at a Glance
Word 2.0 for Windows at a Glance
WordPerfect 6.0 at a Glance
WordPerfect 6.0 for Windows
at a Glance

Call Wordware Publishing, Inc. for names of the bookstores in your area
(214) 423-0090